SAN DIEGO PUBLIC LIBRARY
3 1336 02866 2238

D0021379

# JOHN MILTON

## LITERATURE AND LIFE: BRITISH WRITERS

*Selected list of titles in the series:*

| | |
|---|---|
| W. H. Auden | Wendell Stacy Johnson |
| Jane Austen | June Dwyer |
| Anthony Burgess | Samuel Coale |
| Noel Coward | Robert F. Kiernan |
| Arthur Conan Doyle | Don Richard Cox |
| Ford Madox Ford | Sondra J. Stang |
| E. M. Forster | Claude J. Summers |
| Oliver Goldsmith and Richard Brinsley Sheridan | Marlies K. Danziger |
| Robert Graves | Katherine Snipes |
| Graham Greene | Richard Kelly |
| Aldous Huxley | Guinevera A. Nance |
| Christopher Isherwood | Claude J. Summers |
| James Joyce | Bernard Benstock |
| D. H. Lawrence | George J. Becker |
| Christopher Marlowe | Gerald Pinciss |
| Katherine Mansfield | Rhoda B. Nathan |
| John Masefield | June Dwyer |
| W. Somerset Maugham | Archie K. Loss |
| V. S. Naipaul | Richard Kelly |
| Barbara Pym | Robert Emmet Long |
| Jean Rhys | Arnold E. Davidson |
| Shakespeare's Comedies | Jack A. Vaughn |
| Shakespeare's Histories | George J. Becker |
| Shakespeare's Tragedies | Phyllis Rackin |
| Muriel Spark | Velma Bourgeois Richmond |
| Tom Stoppard | Felicia Londré |
| J. R. R. Tolkien | Katharyn W. Crabbe |
| Evelyn Waugh | Katharyn W. Crabbe |
| H. G. Wells | Brian Murray |
| Oscar Wilde | Robert Keith Miller |
| Virginia Woolf | Manly Johnson |
| William Butler Yeats (Plays) | Anthony Bradley |
| The Poetry of William Butler Yeats | William H. O'Donnell |

Complete list of titles in the series available from the publisher on request

# JOHN MILTON

*Gerald J. Schiffhorst*

*A Frederick Ungar Book*
CONTINUUM • NEW YORK

**For Lynn**

**"Wisest, virtuousest, discreetest, best"**

(*Paradise Lost* 8.550)

1990

The Continuum Publishing Company
370 Lexington Avenue
New York, NY 10017



Printed in the United States of America

**Library of Congress Cataloging-in-Publication Data**

Schiffhorst, Gerald J.
John Milton / Gerald J. Schiffhorst.
p. cm. — (Literature and life series)
"A Frederick Ungar book."
Includes bibliographical references.
ISBN 0–8264–0459–6
1. Milton, John, 1608–1674. 2. Poets, English—Early modern, 1500–1700—Biography. I. Title. II. Series.
PR3581.S34 1990
821'.4—dc20
[B] 89–27922
CIP

# Contents

# Preface

Adding to the innumerable books on Milton might seem gratuitous were it not that few of these studies are intended for the student or other reader confronting this major English poet for the first time. In keeping with the general purpose of the Literature and Life series, I provide a critical introduction to Milton's principal poetry for such readers by placing the poet in the context of seventeenth-century England and by relating his work to the predominant literary traditions that he assimilated. The book shows that Milton the poet and Milton the politician are inseparable. It sees him as a romantic visionary whose personal and political struggles make him remarkable both for his artistic originality and for his positive, hopeful view of human nature. As an idealist, Milton has answers to the timeless mysteries of life, yet as a realist he asks as many fundamental questions as he answers, and the questions are often as provocative.

I have included reproductions of representative works of art not only as analogues to the poetry but also as reminders of Milton's indebtedness to, and influence on, the visual arts. I am grateful to the Prado (Madrid) for permission to reproduce *The Fall* by Rubens; to the Henry E. Huntington Library and Art Gallery for permission to reproduce *Satan, Sin and Death* by Blake; and to the Princeton University Library for permission to reproduce (on the jacket) Faithorne's portrait of Milton.

Every writer on Milton owes an accumulated debt of gratitude to countless scholars, living and dead. The work of R. M. Frye, M. Y. Hughes, L. L. Martz, B. Rajan, J. M. Steadman, and J. H. Summers has been especially valuable to me, and my indebtedness to their insights and to those of Stanley Fish, Anthony Low, and Harry Blamires extends well beyond what the documentation can indicate. My citations for Milton's poetry are from *John Milton: Complete Poetry and Major Prose,* ed. M. Y. Hughes (New York: Odyssey, 1957). Quotations from the prose are from *The Complete Prose Works of John Milton,* 8 vols., ed. D. M. Wolfe et al. (New Haven: Yale University Press and London: Oxford University Press, 1953–82).

I have benefited from the generous advice of Albert C. Labriola, who read an earlier draft of several chapters and offered invaluable advice. The University of Central Florida provided me with research aid, and I was fortunate to have in Russell Kesler a student assistant who performed duties large and small with uncommon dedication and insight. I am grateful to Bea Stewart for preparing the manuscript with great skill and patience. My colleague and friend Jerome Donnelly has, as always, provided encouragement and important suggestions. My greatest debt, as registered in the dedication, is to my wife, Lynn Butler Schiffhorst, for being the best possible reader and source of support.

Orlando, Florida
July 1989

# Chronology

| | |
|---|---|
| 1608 | John Milton is born in Cheapside, London, on December 9, the eldest son of John Milton, a well-to-do scrivener, and Sarah Jeffrey Milton. |
| 1618–20 | Tutored privately by Thomas Young. |
| 1620–25 | Attends St. Paul's School, London, where the humanist curriculum of Latin and Greek is combined with Christian piety. There Milton meets his closest friend, Charles Diodati, and reads the works of Edmund Spenser and Guillaume du Bartas. |
| 1625 | Admitted to Christ's College, Cambridge, where he is to spend seven years. At Cambridge, he is called "The Lady of Christ's" because of his chaste aloofness. He writes Italian and Latin poems and has a row with his tutor. Studies music, mathematics, history, and geography, and adds Hebrew to his knowledge of Latin, Greek, French, and Italian. |
| 1629 | Receives BA on March 26. Writes "Ode on the Morning of Christ's Nativity." Charles I dissolves Parliament and attempts to govern alone. |
| 1629–32 | Continues studies for MA, which he receives on July 3, 1632. "The Passion," Italian sonnets, *Arcades,* "On Time," "At a Solemn Music," "L'Allegro," and "Il Penseroso" belong to this period. |
| 1631 | Begins ambitious reading program in Hammersmith, living with his parents in rural isolation. Writes sonnet, "How Soon Hath Time." |

| | |
|---|---|
| 1632 | Invited to contribute a poem to the second folio of Shakespeare's plays, edited by Ben Jonson. |
| 1634 | *Comus* performed in Ludlow Castle on September 29, written in collaboration with composer Henry Lawes for the inauguration of the Earl of Bridgewater as The Lord President of Wales, following an earlier collaboration with Lawes on *Arcades*. |
| 1635 | Milton moves with his parents to Horton, near Windsor, where he continues his private studies, totaling nearly six years' study of literature, history, philosophy, science, mathematics, and music. |
| 1637 | Milton's mother dies. *Comus* published by Henry Lawes. Following the death of Edward King, Milton writes "Lycidas," which is published in a 1638 collection of poems, *Justa Eduardo King*. |
| 1638–39 | Fifteen months of travel, mostly in Italy, including visits with Galileo and Manso. Lavish praise of his poetry by Italian humanists and a reinforcing of his Protestant sympathies. Returns with new desire to achieve poetic fame. |
| 1639 | Back in London, begins tutoring nephews, Edward and John Phillips, in his home in Aldersgate. |
| 1640 | Undertakes the study of Christian doctrine. Writes prose works opposing bishops. Publishes *Epitaphium Damonis*, a Latin elegy on his friend Charles Diodati. Long Parliament meets. |
| 1641 | Anonymous publication of the first of five antiprelatical pamphlets, *Of Reformation* and *Apology for Smectymnuus*. |
| 1642 | Marries Mary Powell; publishes *Reason of Church Government*. In late summer Mary returns to her parents' home in Oxfordshire. Civil War begins August 22. Royalist army establishes headquarters in Oxford. |
| 1643 | Milton publishes *Doctrine and Discipline of Divorce*, followed by other divorce pamphlets in 1644 and 1645, producing controversy and notoriety. |

1644 His eyesight begins to fail. Writes *Areopagitica,* an eloquent defense of freedom of expression, and *Of Education,* which proposes an idealistic humanist curriculum for his hoped-for liberal commonwealth. Conducts small school in his London house. Royalist Forces suffer defeat at Marston Moor.

1645 Reunited with Mary, Milton moves to a larger house to accommodate pupils and relatives. His first volume of collected poems is published, with little critical acclaim. Publishes *Tetrachordon.*

1646 First daughter, Anne, is born on July 29. First Civil War ends with king's surrender. Milton takes in Royalist in-laws.

1647 Deaths of Milton's father and father-in-law.

1648 Daughter Mary is born on October 25. Second Civil War begins.

1649 Execution of Charles I on January 30. Commonwealth proclaimed. Milton appointed Secretary for Foreign Languages, a translator of letters for the Council of State in the Cromwell government. Publishes *On the Tenure of Kings and Magistrates* and *Eikonoklastes,* written in response to *Eikon Basilike,* supposedly composed by the king.

1651 Only son John is born on March 16. *Pro Populo Anglicano Defensio* (A Defense of the English People) is published to vindicate the Commonwealth abroad. This document ruined the career of his opponent, the noted scholar Claudius Salmasius, and impaired his own health.

1652 Milton's blindness becomes complete. Daughter, Deborah, is born on May 2, and wife Mary dies on May 5. Son dies on June 16. *Samson Agonistes* may have been begun about this time.

1653 Cromwell dissolves Rump Parliament and begins Protectorate.

1654 *Defensio Secunda pro Populo Anglicano* (Second Defense) published, in which Milton defends himself against many personal attacks and reveals much about his feelings.

1655 *Pro Se Defensio* (Defense of Himself) published; most of the sonnets completed. Milton relieved of principal government duties.

1656 Milton marries Katherine Woodcock and begins composition of *Christian Doctrine,* his private reflections on religion in Latin, published in 1825.

1657 Daughter, Katherine, born on October 19. Second Protectorate begins.

1658 Katherine Woodcock and daughter, Katherine, die. Last sonnet (no. 23) written. *Paradise Lost* perhaps begun this year. Cromwell dies.

1659 *Treatise of Civil Power* and *Means to Remove Hirelings out of the Church* published.

1660 With the Restoration of the monarchy under Charles II, Milton is dismissed from his secretaryship. In June, Parliament issues warrant for Milton's arrest and orders copies of his works burned; is briefly detained, then aided by his brother Christopher and by Andrew Marvell. *A Ready and Easy Way to Establish a Free Commonwealth* published.

1663 Marries Elizabeth Minshull, his third wife, who proves to be a greater help than his daughters Mary and Deborah as he composes *Paradise Lost.* Despite fame and foreign visitors, he lives in relative poverty and isolation in London.

1665 Resides briefly in Chalfont St. Giles to escape plague.

1667 *Paradise Lost: A Poem Written in Ten Books* published.

1671 *History of Britain* published. *Paradise Regained* and *Samson Agonistes* published together.

1673 *Of True Religion* and a new edition of collected poems published.

1674 Milton dies of gout in London on November 8. Is buried at St. Giles, Cripplegate, after elaborate funeral attended by John Dryden and other notable figures. The second edition of *Paradise Lost,* now in twelve books, published. Latin Prolusions (1628–32) published.

1682 *A Brief History of Moscovia* published, attesting to Milton's long interest in geography and history.

1825 *De Doctrina Christiana (Christian Doctrine)* published.

# 1

# Milton's Life and Times

John Milton has been the subject of more commentary than any other English writer with the exception of Shakespeare. Reading his work is itself a humanizing education, for he expects us to know both the Bible (and theological commentary on it) and the ancient classics that inspired him from precocious boyhood to serene old age. A poet as well as an amateur musician and theologian, Milton read widely in virtually every field of knowledge and was actively engaged in the politics of his time As the last Renaissance Christian humanist, he could justifiably claim to know most of what could be known, to embrace both past and present, the natural and the supernatural, and view it all coherently. In Milton's era, knowledge was supported by ancient authorities (classical, medieval, mythological) yet was increasingly subject to recent scientific discoveries. In the seventeenth century, as Basil Willey has observed, the walls of separation between reason and faith, science and classical learning, mythology and the Bible, sacred and profane love, action and contemplation "were only beginning to be made which for later ages shut off poetry from science, metaphor from fact."[1] In Milton these areas were not separated but interrelated, and art based on classical models was for him a means of encouraging a life of Christian virtue. Thus, while aware of the scientific advancements of his own age, Milton was also the last major English poet to draw upon the same ideas that had influenced Chaucer and Shakespeare.

A towering figure in an especially prolific period, he stood apart from its fashionable literary styles yet was passionately engaged in its public issues. Milton, who seems to us traditional, was in fact a radical independent, both in literature and in politics. As an experimental poet, he transformed every genre he used—the elegy, sonnet, masque, epic, drama—and forged a new synthesis between the classical past and contemporary Christianity in a style uniquely his. According to Christopher Hill, Milton "is the greatest English revolutionary who is also a poet, the greatest English poet who is also a revolutionary."[2] Though his political and religious views may seem remote to us, he was a strong champion of liberty who argued for divorce and for freedom of the press. Many readers, considering only his public persona, have found him vain, humorless, bigoted, and elitist; yet Milton the man could be witty, sensitive, compassionate, and capable of great spiritual strength amid adversity. He remains a complex, controversial figure who was confident that posterity would remember him as a man of reason and destiny. Convinced that his blindness set him apart from others, he saw himself as a divinely ordained poet-seer in the company of Homer, Tiresias, and Samson, with an obstinate faith in himself and in the rightness of his cause.

The London into which John Milton was born on December 9, 1608, and where he would spend nearly all his life, was a rapidly growing metropolis. The population of more than 200,000 would double by 1660. Not far from the Milton family home in Cheapside was the Mermaid Tavern, where Shakespeare, Ben Jonson, and other playwrights and poets gathered. It was an eventful, colorful time in post-Elizabethan England: during Milton's boyhood, theater enjoyed its golden age, music flourished, John Donne, Francis Bacon, and other great writers were doing some of their most important work, and the translation known as the King James Bible was published (in 1611). The king, who had succeeded Queen Elizabeth I in 1603, had already upset the growing body of Puritans within the Church of England with his declaration of Stuart policy, "No bishop, no king," for they believed, as would Milton, that the Reformation and religious freedom would not be possible in England without the abolition of the state-related episcopacy.

Religious nonconformity was part of Milton's upbringing, his father having been disinherited for turning Protestant. John Milton, the poet's father, left his Catholic Oxfordshire family to make his fortune in London as a scrivener (moneylender and lawyer) and was able to give his eldest son the best education that an upper-middle-class family could provide. The senior Milton was also an accomplished composer who introduced his son to music as well as books. Their house on Bread Street, in the shadow of old St. Paul's Cathedral, was located in an overcrowded, squalid area, but it afforded young John a cultivated home where he studied with a private tutor, a clergyman named Thomas Young. He grew up in an atmosphere that respected piety and religious independence. He was taught to sing and play the organ. And, from an early age, he was especially studious and brilliant. In a later prose work, he wrote (in Latin):

> My father destined me from childhood to the study of humane letters, and I took to those studies with such ardor that, from the time I was twelve, I hardly ever gave up reading for bed until midnight. This was the first cause of injury to my eyes, which were naturally weak, and I suffered from many headaches.

Milton went to St. Paul's School near his home; there, most probably, he was introduced to English poetry, including Sylvester's translation of Guillaume Du Bartas's *Divine Weeks and Works,* a poetic rendering of the Creation and related biblical stories. There he also read the work of the poet who was to become his principal inspiration: Edmund Spenser's *The Faerie Queene* (1590). "Spenser's preoccupations—Platonic idealism, classical mythology, medieval legend, militant Protestantism dressed in the most Italianate poetic forms—filled Milton's head while he was still a boy at St. Paul's."[3] But the curriculum was largely the conventional trivium—grammar, rhetoric, and logic—and was intended to teach Latin thoroughly as a second native language, for it was not only the international medium of expression but also the key to ancient and contemporary knowledge. Classical Latin and Greek necessarily involved the study of history, poetry, philosophy, oratory, and drama as well. Christian principles were also firmly inculcated at St. Paul's, and Milton always valued the solid grounding in humanistic learning provided there. Nothing of the scrupulous spirit of Puritanism so influential in Milton's century affected his humanist education at St. Paul's, with its enthusiastic acceptance of every aspect of literature and learning, its intense and thorough curriculum. This approach to education helps us understand Milton's sophisticated Latin juvenilia without regarding him as a nearly monstrous prodigy.

Equally valuable were Milton's school ties. He enjoyed an adolescence with a coterie of appreciative, like-minded boys who scorned less cultivated minds. He became the close friend of another bright boy, Charles Diodati, the grandson of Italian Protestants, whose knowledge of Italian no doubt influenced Milton's mastery of this language; he also learned Latin, Greek, French, and Hebrew. His great devotion to Diodati is reflected in several youthful Latin Poems, and their friendship was to be the only such intimate, fulfilling relationship in Milton's life. A more intellectual bond was established with the outgoing son of the headmaster, Alexander Gill, whose poetry and anti-Stuart views influenced Milton. His later friendship with Edward King, celebrated in "Lycidas," was no doubt mingled with nostalgic memories of his associations with Diodati and Gill as well as with his pleasant memories of St. Paul's.

The young Milton was elegantly refined, somewhat effeminate in appearance, always aware of his superior abilities but also aware of his slow development ("I do notice a certain belatedness in me"). When he entered Cambridge at sixteen, the delicate, handsome, auburn-haired youth, known for his chastity and aloofness, was nicknamed "The Lady of Christ's College." He had additional reasons for disliking the university: He found the lectures boring and repetitious, given his rigorous early preparation at home and school, and the atmosphere provincial in contrast to that of London. Yet he seems to have been respected among the undergraduates for being boisterous as well as scholarly since he was invited to speak at several raucous functions where he displayed his satirical wit. At age seventeen, he fancied himself both a poet and a ladies' man. Ill at ease in expressing his feelings in English, he wrote of his infatuation with a girl named Emilia in an Italian sonnet. He fell in love easily but remained emotionally shy, and his determination to achieve fame as a poet took precedence over love and marriage. Though his father expected him to enter the Church, Milton was not impressed by the boorish Cambridge students preparing for the ministry; more important, he was hostile to the established church and was determined to be a poet. Early on, he viewed himself in the company of the great classical writers.

Scholars do not agree whether a misunderstanding with his first tutor, William Chapell, resulted in Milton's being "sent down" (dismissed) for part of his first year at Cambridge or whether (as is more likely) he merely left briefly after a row with Chapell, frustrated by a stale curriculum that taught him nothing new. In any case, he returned to the university and received his BA in 1629; he was first among the honors graduates of his college, as he was again in 1632, when he received his Master of Arts degree. His studies included languages, music, mathematics, history, and geography. Teaching consisted of lectures, mostly in Latin, and public disputations or debates (Milton's Prolusions) in which the student had to defend a standard proposition ("whether day or night is more excellent") to display his rhetorical skills. Milton seems to have enjoyed the opportunity for wit and sarcasm offered by these exercises, even though he found them irrelevant to serious study, and later published some of them, complete with bawdy humor. The Prolusions reflect a taste for debate central to many of the poet's major works.

By his twenty-fifth birthday, Milton had been a poet for ten years, often preferring to express his poetic feelings tentatively in impersonal Latin rather than in the less worthy vernacular. He had begun with some English paraphrases of the Psalms. There followed several Latin elegies, Italian sonnets, and English poems in the style of Spenser. Although he had no need to earn money, he lacked a profession and was concerned, as Sonnet 7 reveals, about wasting his talents. He considered the idea of marriage but felt that a celibate life would best suit his higher poetic calling since he felt that he had a divine mission. As a result, he decided that his life should become a work of art—dedicated, disciplined, virtuous, and well planned. For nearly six years he joined his parents in their retirement, first at Hammersmith, then at Horton (seventeen miles from London). There, despite his father's misgivings about Milton's lack of a career, he settled down for a period of intense, systematic study of literature, history, philosophy, science, music, and mathematics. His aim was to master all learning, to become the ideal Renaissance humanist who could one day write immortal verse. During these important years, he also found intellectual support for his liberal political and religious ideas. Yet, in this isolated stay in the country, apart from the burgeoning careers of his contemporaries, he could hardly escape feeling at loose ends, wondering whether the advice of his old tutor Thomas Young—to avoid mere study and withdrawal from life—was not right. So, if he was not to enter the church, he would dedicate himself to God's service through art, confident that in time he would be fit for a poetic priesthood.

His revealing poem to his father, "Ad Patrem" (c. 1634) shows, despite obvious paternal disagreement over a poetic career for the younger Milton, affection, gratitude, and a sense of independence. The poet requests further leisure for his studies and defends his need to study, preferring not to enter business or the "noisy stupidity" of the law courts. The poem also provides the earliest account of Milton's dedication to poetry. Second only to his commitment to God, and related to it, is his dominant sense of his destiny to be a great poet who could contribute to the glory of God and the public good. His writing, then, stems not from vanity but from high-minded aspiration; he sees himself as a man of great talent and views poetry, as he later wrote, as capable of cultivating "in a great people the seeds of virtue." To become such an inspired poet-preacher required an extensive education as well as the lofty idealism we see expressed in his correspondence with Diodati, with whom he enjoyed learned, philosophical talk along with a cultivated contempt for mediocrity and "the base opinion of common men." Thus we see recurring in Milton's character a desire for fame coupled with a sense of isolated aloofness, even hostility toward the masses. In 1642, he spoke of himself as reserved and fastidious with an "honest haughtiness and self-esteem."

Like Shakespeare, Donne, Jonson, and other leading poets of the time, Milton sought aristocratic patronage. The prominent musician and friend of the Miltons, Henry Lawes, was to produce a masque for the Dowager Countess of Derby. Milton wrote the text and called it *Arcades*. Masques had become popular, elaborate court entertainments, combining music, dance, and spectacle with some allegorical or mythological story. A more important commission for the same family (and another collaboration with Lawes) resulted in the lovely philosophical masque, *Comus*, presented at Ludlow Castle in 1634. Like most masques, *Comus* celebrates the virtues of an aristocratic family; more particularly, this pastoral work emphasizes the beauty of chastity in Platonic terms. The success of the masque—it became a popular opera a century later—did not result in any further patronage or court appointment, as Milton perhaps hoped. So he returned to solitude, prayer, and study, "the curious search into knowledge," as Milton's nephew wrote after his death, being "the grand affair perpetually of his life."

Amid his peaceful studies, Milton wrote to Diodati and other friends that his self-absorbed program of reading was purposeful even if he did not seek advancement in the church. He was, as always, confident of his own genius and destiny, sensing that he was capable of greater things but that his time had not come. He planned various ambitious projects: a definitive history of England, a Latin-English dictionary, and works on logic and theology as well as poetry and drama. Then, a few months after his mother's death, Milton learned of the drowning of Edward King, whom he had known since Cambridge. When asked to contribute an elegy to a memorial volume, he chose the pastoral mode of Spenser and produced what most critics consider one of the greatest of English lyrics, "Lycidas." In this work Milton typically transcends the occasion, treating himself more than King and universalizing his grief in an elaborately allusive poem. His attack in the elegy on corrupt clergy expresses his hope that the Church of England will reform itself from within.

At twenty-nine, having completed a small but significant body of poetry, Milton set out with a manservant for Italy on one of the great educational journeys in literary history. His fifteen months on the Continent sharpened his Protestant sympathies and strengthened his chauvinistic, idealistic belief in England as a divinely appointed place that should lead Europe in completing the Reformation. The paintings and buildings he saw influenced his later imagery in *Paradise Lost*. He would especially retain the memory of persons and places he visited during long stays in Florence and Rome, especially of the blind scientist Galileo, under house arrest. Milton's lifelong political opposition to Catholicism did not prevent him from enjoying the company and friendship of Catholics, including Cardinal Barberini, the humanists Giovanni Battista Manso and Carlo Dati, and the Vatican librarian. Italian scholars hailed his poetry, giving him the recognition that had largely eluded him in England. His command of Italian must have been excellent, for the Florentines were lavish in their praise of the young English poet. While in Italy, he wrote several Latin poems that reveal a new self-confidence; one, in praise of Manso, mentions plans for a heroic poem on King Arthur.

Growing church-state troubles back home caused him to shorten his journey. Stopping in Geneva on the return trip, he learned of the death of his closest friend, Diodati; his later Latin elegy for Diodati, *Epitaphium Damonis,* his most emotional poem, marks the end of his youth, the beginning of a more somber awareness of mortality. His European experience had some unexpected political consequences: Milton's anti-Royalist attitudes became crystallized. But he did not become politically active at once, waiting until the climate was right for him to express radical positions publicly. The Italian journey also contributed to Milton's musical interests; he shipped home "a chest or two of choice music books," including works by Monteverdi. Travel, reading, and the cultivation of learned and aristocratic friends had been part of his preparation to achieve poetic fame, an ambition furthered by his being so enthusiastically received in Italy.

He returned to London, where he helped to raise and educate his two nephews, John and Edward Phillips (sons of his sister Anne), while considering the idea of writing a national epic in the vernacular, as the Italian poets had done. England in that summer of 1639 was poised for war. King Charles I (1625–49) increased the hostility between various Puritan groups and those loyal to the crown (the Royalists) by a series of disastrous policies: forcing uniform services on the divided Church of England, insisting on what he considered God-given rights as king, and marrying a Catholic princess. Like his father, James I, Charles failed to appreciate the role of Parliament, the rise of the middle class, and the people's religious sensibilities. The church, badly split between Puritan reformers (Independents, Presbyterians, Anabaptists, and other sects) and Anglicans, had been at the center of decades of unrest, hostility, and censorship, causing some of the radical reformers to leave for New England. The Protestants who stayed insisted, not on the compromises offered by the king, but on a purgation of the old Catholic hierarchical and liturgical system. They advocated a simple, democratic church that would allow each person to interpret scripture according to his or her own conscience. Tradition, ritual, and church structure, they said, should be reformed and bishops stripped of their power.

From the perspective of the mid-seventeenth century, Crown and Parliament were seen as having been in harmony during the

Elizabethan age; the episcopate and the monarchy then seemed destined to lead the worldwide Protestant cause. But under the Stuart kings James and Charles, with their absolutist tendencies and pro-Catholic leanings, the chance for England to fulfill her part in the divine plan of history seemed lost. Radicals began to see bishops as obstacles to the Reformation, not champions of it. Moreover, the endowed state church with its lord bishops represented for Milton and his contemporaries a further corruption of primitive Christianity, which was thought to have declined soon after the time of the Apostles. For Milton, the gospel, not the church, is everlasting; there is, he contended, no legitimate church on earth, only individuals, who should not band together into organized churches but wait patiently for God to redeem Christianity's long "flight into the wilderness" caused by "the perverse iniquity of 1600 years."

The English Civil War (1642–48) between King Charles I and the parliamentarians has been called the Puritan Revolution because the king's opponents were comprised of various Puritan factions opposed to bishops in the Church of England and because the king's defeat was accompanied by the abolition of the episcopacy. But the essential, constitutional conflict was between a king who claimed to rule by divine right and a Parliament that claimed sovereignty independent of the crown. Opposition to the monarchy by Parliament's sizable middle class (gentry and merchants) during the reign of James I (1603–25) grew under his son, Charles, whose powers the parliamentary party sought to limit.

Charles, believing he allowed the people as much freedom as they needed, was a timid man and an ineffectual politician but not, as his adversaries claimed, a tyrant who broke faith with his subjects by waging war against them. When the episcopal system of church government and the Anglican Prayer Book were forced on Scotland, Parliament and popular sympathy joined to oppose the king. This Scottish policy was the work of the Archbishop of Canterbury, William Laud, who attempted to link loyalty to the throne with loyalty to the state church. In appointing many bishops to secular posts, elevating the status of the clergy, and advocating censorship, Laud angered many Englishmen. In trying to reform the church, Laud sought to eliminate the many Protestant sects in England in favor of one episcopal church. His unpopularity with Puritans as well as Anglicans added to Charles's unpopularity as well.

Before the Civil War the king's disastrous Scottish policy led to sympathy for the Presbyterians, those who advocated that elders replace bishops in governing the church. When the war began, the parliamentary forces believed that the conflict would result in Charles's heading a Presbyterian state church, as in Scotland. But the Presbyterian system could not be affected in England, and the Presbyterians hated the smaller sects more than the Anglican church they had rebelled against. Their chief opponents were the Independents, men like Milton who advocated religious toleration and opposed any established church.

In 1629, Parliament protested the king's collection of customs duties as well as the prosecution of his opponents. Charles tried to rule for the following decade without a Parliament. In 1639, battles in Scotland over the imposition of Laud's Anglican policy forced Charles to seek Parliament's financial aid. When Parliament insisted on discussing more fundamental issues, the king dissolved Parliament after three weeks. The disasters of the war in Scotland forced the king's virtual surrender to the opposition, and the Long Parliament, beginning in 1640, enacted measures to end royal encroachments on its authority. The Star Chamber, long a source of royal power in church matters, was abolished, but agreement could not be reached on church reform. Radical demands split the parliamentary party and caused some moderates to join the Royalist cause. Encouraged by this, Charles in 1642 tried to arrest several opposition leaders, an action making civil war inevitable. After the inconclusive battle of Edgehill, Charles established headquarters in Oxford; his forces gained ground in the north and west, but attempts to advance on London were futile. In 1643, Oliver Cromwell emerged to military prominence with his own regiment, but the skirmishes were inconclusive. Parliament, to secure Scottish aid, promised to submit England to Presbyterianism, an action that led to dissension among parliamentary leaders.

The degree to which the King failed to see that he had already been defeated partially explains the duration of the war. And it is further explained when one considers that it was one of the most half-hearted wars in history. It only occupied the attentions of a small proportion of the population. It did not divide the nation entirely between ardent supporters of one side or another. On the contrary, most either did not know it was going on, or were angry with both sides for being unable to resolve their differences peaceably.[4]

The Royalist forces were crushed in the decisive battle of Marston Moor in 1644. A year later, the Royalist cause was hopeless. The first phase of the Civil War ended in 1646 when Charles surrendered himself to the Scots, who later delivered him to Parliament. The Presbyterian rule in that body had alienated the army, under the command of Thomas Fairfax, which resisted Parliament's proposal to disband it by capturing the king from the Parliamentary party and marching on London. Charles, refusing to accept the radical army council's proposals for peace, escaped in 1647 to the Isle of Wight, where he made an agreement with the Scots to accept Presbyterianism in return for military support. In 1648, the second Civil War began and ended quickly with the Scots defeated by Cromwell. The conflict in the second phase of the war was between Independents, who comprised the bulk of the New Model Army under Cromwell, and the largely Presbyterian Parliament, which continued to advocate a state church and negotiations with the king. The Independent forces defeated the Presbyterian army in 1648 and took control of Parliament. Thus a minority faction, not reflecting popular feeling, dominated Parliament. The Rump Parliament tried the king for treason and ordered his execution, which occurred in London on January 30, 1649. A republic known as the Commonwealth was set up, followed by the Protectorate, both marked by Cromwell's strict military rule.

Forced to choose between no state church and a Presbyterian state church, the revolutionary governments chose the latter, despite Milton's urgings. Cromwell and the Commonwealth were more conservative than Milton and afraid to support more radical groups. The revolution thus failed to win supporters on left or right and failed by replacing what its leaders saw as episcopal tyranny with their own tyranny. Fear of social and economic anarchy led to the restoration of the Church of England and the monarchy in 1660.

Milton, long opposed to what he considered episcopal tyranny, was ready to enter the fray in 1640, convinced that the first step in restoring the church to its ancient simplicity was to abolish the bishops and church ritual, which he was to call "the new-vomited paganism of sensual idolatry." Such language, engaged in by all sides in the long dispute, may seem out of keeping with the standard image of Milton the sober Puritan, yet this stereotyped image obscures the real political partisan, who began his public career with a keen sense of wanting to be noticed. He joined the fight with such ruthless energy and passionate conviction that we cannot help but be struck by the way such writing reveals Milton's own psyche and concern with himself.

The prose works, along with the sonnets of the same period, reflect the experience of Milton's middle years (1641–60) and reveal the personality of a writer who relished controversy and conflict. He called the prose works achievements of "my left hand," recognizing that his true artistry was reserved for poetry. Yet, more than others involved in the parliamentary struggles, he wrote with an intensity of feeling that added considerable power to the political debate of the time. Entering the public arena more to dictate than to participate, Milton saw the conflict in broad terms, with no room for compromise: The episcopacy was an abstract evil, a parasite destroying the nation. Despite the inescapable egotism apparent in these works and their mixture of lofty ideals with often harsh rhetoric, the reader is often dazzled by the power of the writing, with its rich vocabulary, its lively metaphors, its flashes of wit and colloquial freshness. The magniloquent lyricism of the early prose gives way, however, to increasing vindictiveness and a more sober style as Milton adjusts to the changing political climate. He remains straightforward in stating his own worth and in defending himself, often with "more regard for victory than for the fairness of the details used."[5] Such tactics and exaggeration might be expected, given the heated political and religious climate in which propagandists tended to reveal more about what could best be argued than about what they actually believed. Along with the sonnets, Milton's prose works reveal much about the poet's thought and character during his public years when the seeds of the great poems of struggle and temptation were germinating.

Not an original political thinker, Milton was greatly influenced by the English Revolution in which he actively participated. He synthesized ideas gleaned from books as well as from discussions with his contemporaries. Thus the evolution of the poet's ideas is linked to the development of radical Protestant thinking that rejected traditional Calvinist orthodoxy along with belief in the Trinity. In the various heresies being preached, Milton shared an interest with the confusing variety of sects (Levelers, Diggers, Ranters, Seekers, Baptists, Quakers, among others) that consisted of what Hill describes as a lively, popular radical underground. Milton's response to this welter of opinion was to return to his own study of the Bible and to develop his own conclusions in what would become the *Christian Doctrine*.

In five antiepiscopal tracts published in 1641–42, Milton wrestled with the nature of institutional Christianity, wondering if there was adequate scriptural basis for bishops and priests. These prose works, reflecting long-held, deeply felt positions, reveal his belief in religious freedom, which he saw as inseparable from the abolition of the bishops; as his visit to Italy confirmed, this system had political implications that impaired freedom of thought. If the Church of England, to which Milton always nominally belonged, would adopt a presbyterian type of organization, he felt, it could lead the way to a discovery of virtue as he had found it in the classics of the ancient world.

Milton's antiprelatical pamphlets reflect the belief that England should take the lead in completing the Reformation, which, he said, had "struck through the black and settled night of ignorance and antichristian tyranny." Milton expressed more strongly and eloquently than others a popular Protestant point of view: that the true church had continued to flourish in England because of an ongoing tradition of reform, part of "an unfolding divine purpose for England and so for the world."[6] Milton's public role was not strictly political, for he was not concerned with politicians or the details of implementing policy; the issue between king and Parliament, as he saw it, was part of a great, historic, religious drama involving the victory of Protestantism and the preparation for the Second Coming. Milton shared in the prophetic view of divinely ordained history propounded by Protestants who held that the fall of the Antichrist would result in a new age of enlightenment preparatory to the millennium. He also believed in the very different classical tradition of ancient freedom and civil humanism, including an aristocracy of the virtuous elite. This ideal, with its republican political implications, Milton tried to unite with the theocratic view of history, producing, according to Hugh Trevor-Roper, an inherent contradiction. "No other man combined with such intensity the two ill-assorted ideals of millennial Puritanism and classical liberty."[7]

Most of Milton's sonnets were written when much of his energy was devoted to the composition of his political pamphlets.* Although not a prolific sonneteer, Milton was a master of the sonnet form whose innovations reveal that a great poet can extend, rather than be limited by, such a restricted form. Milton rejected the Petrarchan conventions of most English sonneteers, which demanded that thought and structure be related and that the poem have love as its subject. In reading Tasso and other Italian poets, Milton realized that the sonnet need not be a love poem but can be used to express public feeling in distinctive, innovative verse, transcending the arbitrary division of thought into quatrains and tercets. Milton also differed from other Renaissance poets in that he did not use the sonnet to tell a story, each sonnet being rather an entity in itself that relates to a particular experience. Indeed, J. H. Hanford holds that it was Milton, not the Elizabethans, who set the style for the English sonnet at its revival toward the end of the eighteenth century.[8] Milton's sonnets are unique in his poetic canon for their direct and plain style. Hanford has described them this way:

> They are the most immediately personal of all Milton's utterances, representing emotional moments in his later life which find no adequate expression in the prose writing . . . they were, like the Psalms, prompted in part by a conscious desire in Milton to exercise himself in verse in preparation for the epic poem which he still intended.[9]

Milton's political career was marked by controversy, and his attitude toward women has caused almost as much censure as his politics. In thinking of women as inferior to men, he shared the values of his time; but he was not a misogynist. In fact, Hill

*There are eighteen sonnets in English in addition to five in Italian; the latter, along with various Latin poems, belong to the poet's youth.

asserts what other scholars have demonstrated: that Milton's views "were on the whole more favourable to women than those of most of his articulate contemporaries."[10] Milton's advocacy of education for both sexes and his schooling of his daughters suggest that he was more of a feminist than has been recognized. His concern that women not remain in bondage to unjust husbands also supports this view, as does his characterization of Eve in *Paradise Lost:* she begins the reconciliation with Adam and God and is not given primary blame for the Fall. The poet, moreover, always had a keen appreciation of women, as John Carey observes:

> He married three times, and the most moving of his poems mourns the death of his second wife. He enjoyed the company of educated, elegant women like Lady Margaret Ley and Mrs. Catherine Thomason—both remembered in sonnets—and the brilliant young Viscountess Ranelagh. When he was twenty, he fell in love with an Italian girl. . . . As a young man his favorite reading was the delicately lascivious adventures of Ovid and Tibullus. . . . We find his confiding to Diodati at eighteen how he used to lurk in an elm-grove in the London suburbs to spy on the parties of young girls who passed by, and how excited their light-brown hair and the flush of their complexions made him.[11]

In his thirty-fourth year, suddenly and unexpectedly, he fell in love with, and quickly married, Mary Powell, seventeen, who was perhaps eager to escape her large, noisy family for a quieter life. But she must have found Milton's studious life *too* quiet; she went back to her family in the country after three weeks. Mary's return home need not suggest that she was bitterly unhappy, just that the marriage had begun badly. Milton, still teaching his nephews in London, must have seen Mary as a pupil to be civilized. But it is also important to recall the political climate that affected this much-discussed marriage: the Royalist Powells wanted their daughter safely home at a time when the Civil War was heating up; they lived near Oxford, the Royalist headquarters. If the impulsive marriage trapped the couple, so did the national situation. Soon the road between Oxford and London became impassable.

Though concerned about civil liberties, Milton remained detached from involvement in the early years of the Civil War, thinking that the weakened monarchy under siege already constituted a victory. He remained optimistic that the king would abolish bishops and reduce his power by parliamentary means. The noble nation he idealized in his prose works was in chaos, yet, in a seeming display of egotism, he wrote urging Parliament to reform the divorce laws. Milton saw marriage as a contract intended for the good of society; he therefore claimed that to divorce a wife is a man's civil right. When a marriage fails to foster the happiness God intended, he argued, it is not a virtue to endure it for purely legal reasons. Yet, as his later Second Defense shows, the divorce issue for Milton was central to the political struggle for liberty:

> There are, in all, three varieties of liberty without which civilized life is scarcely possible, namely ecclesiastical liberty, domestic or personal liberty and civil liberty. . . . For in vain does he prattle about liberty in assembly and market-place who at home endures the slavery most unworthy of man, slavery to an inferior.

He and Mary seemed forever separated yet bound by vows that neither church nor state could repeal. This separation caused him to consider the then-radical issue of divorce. In his divorce pamphlet, he did not mention his own brief experience of marriage but spoke generally (avoiding any mention of desertion as a grounds for divorce); the result was a best-seller that produced extreme reactions, pro and con. When Parliament moved to censor his work, which many saw as heresy, he responded with an eloquent defense of free expression, *Areopagitica* (1644), one of the greatest achievements in English prose. Although a work of great influence in later times, as our First Amendment and the views of Thomas Jefferson and Oliver Wendell Holmes attest, it eloquently defends freedom of expression, indicating Milton's patriotic optimism as well as the strict censorship in effect when he wrote. The influence of the work down through the centuries, especially on American and French revolutionaries, has been considerable; Milton's doctrine of no prior restraint on what might be published has often been invoked in modern times. Milton's opinion of freedom of expression was not new—he had written in *The Reason of Church Government* of the "honest liberty of a free speech"—and was part of his basic philosophy. Freedom of the press was but the initial issue, allowing Milton to discourse on religious liberty as well as liberty and truth in general. But it is not often recognized that, despite these high ideals, Milton's toleration, when made specific, is strictly limited to people who share his values and ideas. As a Protestant humanist opposed to religious authority, Milton consistently emphasizes the theme that external freedom (from government constraint) depends on internal freedom, responsibility, and virtue. Virtue is an inner discipline and growth that cannot be imposed; he insists that men must exercise free choice amid the conflicting claims of good and evil, a theme central in *Paradise Lost.*

Milton now had something of a small school at home and prepared an important tract, *Of Education,* proposing an ideal humanist curriculum for his hoped-for liberal commonwealth. He also began writing a play, *Adam Unparadised,* the germ of *Paradise Lost.* With his eyes troubling him increasingly, he responded to the vicious attacks on his *Doctrine and Discipline of Divorce* with is own vicious prose. In Mary's absence, Milton courted and apparently planned to marry one of the daughters of a physician named Davis, "a very handsome and witty gentlewoman," according to Edward Phillips. But, perhaps dissuaded by the Powells, the lady refused. Then quite suddenly, three years after she had left, Mary Powell Milton returned to her husband; he was thirty-seven, she twenty-one as they began a seemingly happy life together. Soon his London house was alive with activity; in addition to his nephews and his aged father, there was a baby daughter, the first of three children who would survive him.

In the final lines of *Comus* Milton had written, "Love virtue, she alone is free": this spiritual certainty was to be a constant theme in his life and work as he continued to develop his ideas of freedom. *Of Education* represents another view of liberty that Milton hoped to establish in England. It expresses in idealistic terms the need for a humanistic curriculum that would educate England's future leaders. When he wrote that "the end . . . of learning is to repair the ruin of our first parents," Milton meant that education is intended to produce virtue. The thorough mastery of every conceivable area of knowledge envisioned in this 1644 tract reflects Milton's own ambitious educational program for himself. That this program weakened his eyes was apparent from his youth; by 1644, he realized that he was going blind.

Just before the birth of his first child, Anne, in 1646, national and domestic crises combined to test Milton's patience. After the parliamentary army under Cromwell defeated the king's forces at Oxford, the five members of the Powell family were able to travel to London, where Milton, in a revealingly generous gesture, took his wife's family into his crowded house. This, as Milton wrote, "in the midst of civil war, bloodshed and rapine." In response to the Presbyterian Parliament's continuing advocacy of a state church, Milton urged Cromwell to resist, to save England from the "maw of hireling wolves" (that is, government-funded clergy).

With the defeat and imminent execution of the king (in 1649), Milton must have felt a sense of vindication as his views on religious freedom were more generally accepted. A new government under Cromwell was being formed, and Milton was given his first and only job: Secretary for Foreign Languages, that is, interpreter and adviser who wrote and translated letters for the new Council of State. He used his considerable skills to justify government policy but never really influenced that policy. Among his duties, unpleasant for the author of *Areopagitica,* was some censorship work, but he acted with more tolerance than had the Anglican and Presbyterian authorities earlier in the century. The governing council valued Milton's rhetorical skill and was especially impressed by his recent pamphlet, the full title of which reveals its theme:

*The Tenure of Kings and Magistrates; proving, that it is lawful, and hath been so through all ages, for any, who have the power, to call to account a tyrant, or wicked king, and after due conviction, to depose, and put him to death, if the ordinary magistrate have neglected, or denied to do it. And that they who of late, so much blame deposing, are the men that did it themselves.*

The king's execution shocked much of Europe and created instant sympathy for the dead monarch. Milton quickly responded to a volume idealizing the king as a martyr with *Eikonoklastes,* which dutifully defended the republican cause. Despite ill health and failing sight, he then answered another (foreign) defense of monarchy by Europe's leading scholar, Claudius Salmasius. Milton not only enjoyed controversy but the chance to respond, not to some anonymous pamphleteer or to ignorant London readers, but to a worthy, erudite antagonist. Some feared that he would only harm his country's cause, but Milton's angry rebuttal of Salmasius was intended to demonstrate that England was still governed by cultivated men of learning. His years of study had prepared him well for the historic task of defending England against tyranny before the European court of opinion. Since it was assumed that a bad cause could only be defended by a bad person, personal insults, Milton felt, were justifiable, especially since his nation had been insulted. He sarcastically ridiculed Salmasius's learning and in a point-by-point refutation argued again that kings derive their power from a free people and are not above the law, that the people have the right to punish a tyrant. Milton's fervor and love of controversy could easily blind him to certain truths and lead him to ignore Christian charity and the tolerance he preached: he called Salmasius, among other things, a monster, madman, liar, buffoon, pimp, parasite, and filthy swine. The success of the relatively unknown Milton in overcoming the Goliath, Salmasius, strengthened the poet's political reputation.

As his first biographer, his nephew Edward Phillips, later wrote, Salmasius's career and health were ruined by Milton's response; the writing of this *Pro Populo Anglicano Defensio* (1651) seriously impaired Milton's own health. Despite continued confidence in the righteousness of his cause, Milton's Sonnet 19 ("When I Consider") reflects his melancholy sense that God, who had punished the ruthless, reckless King Charles, had plunged the defender of the regicides into darkness. That he also had neglected his poetic calling in the cause of his country deeply troubled Milton, whose 1645 edition of his collected *Poems* had been met with silence rather than acclaim. Except for occasional sonnets, such as to his young friend and student Cyriack Skinner, Milton wrote forty-five prose tracts but no poetry between 1640 and 1660. Had God cast him into utter darkness for neglecting "that one talent which is death to hide"? In Sonnet 22, he writes that he is supported in his blindness by the knowledge that he lost his sight in "liberty's defense, my noble task, / Of which all Europe talks." Adding to his unhappiness was legal and financial wrangling, including a lawsuit by his mother-in-law over property lost during the political upheaval. Meanwhile, her daughter Mary, the mother of three children, gave birth to a fourth, then died at twenty-seven. Six weeks later Milton lost his only son, John; in that same year, 1652, he became totally blind.

With his duties as a civil servant (and salary) reduced because of his failed sight, Milton produced his most virulent and vitriolic prose work, the *Defensio Secunda,* which has been called one of the world's greatest pieces of rhetoric. In it Milton vigorously defends himself against personal attacks provoked by his early political pamphlets, including the accusation that his blindness was a punishment for supporting the regicides. Called by an opponent "a monster horrible, deformed, huge, sightless" after his attack on Salmasius, Milton in his wounded vanity speaks of his own appearance ("my stature is closer to the medium than the small"). But his self-defense as one favored by God becomes inseparable from his defense of England from foreign assaults. He asserts that his blindness has brought him closer to God and that he is guilty of nothing "whose wickedness could . . . invite upon me this supreme misfortune." The success of the republic under Cromwell, he concludes, will clearly indicate that Englishmen enjoy God's special favor. Though Milton never wrote an autobiography, his self-concern in such works gives us a detailed picture of the feelings of the poet turned revolutionary and propagandist. His letters of this period reveal a desperate effort to regain his sight, yet he continued to assert that he gained spiritual comfort by seeing with the eye of the mind. It is understandable how some biographers have seen a parallel between the poet and his blind character Samson.

Profound failures alternated with triumphant successes. "Milton reached a pinnacle of personal fame and success in the years 1649–52, when he was a European figure of heroic magnitude . . . the bitterness of matrimonial failure, the scandal of the divorce pamphlets, would be forgotten as praise poured in from all sides, and as distinguished foreign visitors flocked to see the great John Milton. He moved easily in the highest intellectual and ruling circles of the English republic."[12] But then, as Cromwell's second Protectorate came to resemble a monarchy and as a state church was reinstituted, Milton's faith in the revolution died. After 1653, he was employed only for occasional translations. While completing the bulk of his sonnets and continuing to work on his *Christian Doctrine,* he found solace in the company of several younger friends, who provided him with some amusement in the darkest of times. Among the happy occasions must have been both the visits of foreign visitors and his second marriage to twenty-eight-year-old Katherine Woodcock, whom he valued as a companion and needed housekeeper. Fifteen months later, in 1658, she died in childbirth.

In a period of great personal and political disappointment, Milton remained committed to his principles and was convinced that, at age fifty, the long interruption of his poetic career was over; the purpose of his life remained unchanged: to write a great poem. Probably while working on his Latin theological treatise, wrestling with issues of God's omnipotence, he began the greatest of his works, *Paradise Lost,* having abandoned long-held plans for a tragedy on the fall of man and for a national epic on Britain. With his public controversies largely behind him, the blind poet-prophet could listen to God's voice dictating to him as he attempted to "assert eternal providence and justify the ways of God to men."

With the death of Cromwell and the Restoration (Charles II came to the throne in 1660), Milton had every reason to be fearful. After all, he had publicly defended the execution of the new monarch's father as well as the government that replaced him. In June 1660 Parliament issued a warrant for Milton's arrest and ordered copies of two of his works burned. With many of his friends, hanged, quartered, or disemboweled, he somehow managed to escape, due in part to his blindness. A marked man for four months in hiding, he also had to fear assassination. No doubt his brother Christopher, a Royalist lawyer, helped prevent a trial; certainly his friend, the poet and partisan Andrew Marvell, helped prevent execution in exchange for a month of imprisonment and the payment of a substantial fine. In his new, passive role, Milton apparently behaved with stoic calm and with the inner fortitude he celebrated in *Paradise Lost* and *Samson Agonistes.* One John Garfield no doubt spoke for many Royalists at the time: "I shall leave him under the rod of correction, wherewith God hath evidenced His particular judgment by striking him blind."[13]

Clearly, the greatest disappointment of Milton's life was the Restoration, yet without its occurrence he might never have written his greatest poems. The experience of defeat and disillusion gave him a sense of human weakness that made the epic much more than a learned, theological poem. *Paradise Lost* must have seemed both old-fashioned in the Restoration period—and revolutionary. In writing this epic of nearly eleven thousand lines of blank verse, Milton had moved from external to internal liberty, from national aspiration to a focus on the individual, who can choose evil or create the "paradise within." In explaining God's ways, Milton also succeeded in dramatically explaining human ways. The story of the Fall of Man was philosophically and politically central to the question of human freedom. The freedom of the will was needed to explain how evil could seem to triumph in the world, as it seemed to have with the defeat of the Revolution. Thus Milton wrestles with God's goodness, justice, and omnipotence, man's understanding of God's will, and the emergence of evil, which is attributed to Satan's taking advantage of the freedom given to man. The poet's choice of subject, then, led to the most universal themes imaginable and reflected the failure of the English Revolution and his role in it.

His life was now quieter than it had been for twenty years. With evenings often devoted to young friends, such as Marvell or Skinner, or to playing his father's chamber organ, Milton reserved his days for dictating his epic to various assistants and secretaries. He had some initial help from his daughters Mary and Deborah, but they soon complained of having to read aloud to their father in languages they could not understand; this exacerbated the tension between them and Milton, who wrote that they had been "unkind" and "ungrateful."

Of greater help and companionship was his third wife, Elizabeth Minshull, whom he married in 1663. They shared a love of music and poetry, and it was Betty Minshull, with whom Milton spent his last twelve years, who witnessed the final stages of the composition of *Paradise Lost*. As a famous man, he was visited by foreign travelers and even invited to accept a post by King Charles (he refused on principle), but his final years were spent in relative poverty and obscurity.

As we look back over the busy career of Milton the public figure, we see that his works reveal much about the private man. He was always strongly motivated to fulfill his destiny, with a sense of responsibility for living up to his talents. A well-disciplined man who rose early and worked late, he wrote that "an idle leisure has never pleased me." He was a lifelong walker who took good care of his never-robust health; as a young man he was skilled in fencing. He enjoyed nature, the theater, lively conversation, wine with his dinner, smoking a pipe, and playing the organ and bass viol. His many friendships show him to have been personable, affectionate, and witty. But he was a man who feared loneliness and yearned for approval. He could distinguish between people as symbols, to whom he was often brutally scornful, and as individuals, irrespective of party or religion, to whom he was often cordial and helpful.

In many ways Milton remains a paradoxical personality: he dreamed of scholarly isolation yet sought acclaim; he was a devout Christian who attended no church; he was convinced of the rightness of his ideas yet continually revised and altered them; he was a scholar who used ruthless energy to justify himself, overestimating his political role and influence; he was an idealist whose eagerness to win could justify any unfair method, who could proclaim the need for tolerance in an intolerant way, as his contempt for Catholics, atheists, and the common people attests. And as a poet destined for greatness, he delayed his poetic career and was dissatisfied with the public recognition he received, which was greater than he acknowledged.

Yet it is to his credit that he remained committed to his principal ideals and faced problems and failures with admirable determination and optimism, not brooding about them nor blaming others yet not admitting that his ideas failed to have much impact on society. His failures were considerable. The disastrous three-year marriage to Mary Powell was followed by the failure of his four divorce tracts to alter prevailing practices just as his antiprelatical tracts resulted in no changes in policy. "His efforts to prevent censorship of the press . . . came to nothing in his lifetime."[14] His political pamphlets were largely a lost cause. In 1659–60, for example, Milton addressed Parliament in a ninety-six-page pamphlet arguing that civil magistrates should not use force in religious issues. He then wrote to Parliament on the need to reform the clergy. Both works were ignored. With sentiment building for a return to monarchy, he wrote his tract against kingship, *The Ready and Easy Way*, which was greeted with scornful laughter. Still, he revised his work for a second edition, but the effort was in vain: the monarchy was restored. He was attacked by a writer who wondered why Milton did not give up writing since he had "done it to little or no purpose." To a perfectionist like Milton, sensitive to criticism, such attacks must have been painful; he always set high standards for himself ("Nothing common or mediocre can be tolerated," he had written in his youthful seventh Prolusion) and wrote of man's ultimate goal as a striving for perfection. Yet he continued undeterred, not willing to admit to personal failures, despite circumstances ("though fall'n on evil days"). A lesser man might well have reacted to the defeat of the English Revolution, which Milton had believed to be divinely inspired and to which he had devoted the best years of his life, with hopeless resignation. James Thorpe believes that Milton dealt with disappointments by writing about the failures of characters like Satan or Samson; this "may have been the only way available to him of recognizing his own failures."[15] He believed that future ages would approve of his ideas, and in many instances he was right. With characteristic courage, he felt that afflictions tested his faith ("not to be able to bear blindness," he wrote, "that is miserable"), and he remained convinced of the rightness of the cause for which he had labored. As the early biographer John Toland wrote, Milton found his own reward largely within himself. Though the Restoration pained him, Milton nevertheless could draw some satisfaction from knowing at least that the absolutism of the king had been reduced by Parliament and that bishops were less tyrannical than he had earlier considered them to be.

Yet further misery came that he was unable to see, only feel with helpless anxiety: a terrible plague in 1665, which spared the poet, he felt, to perform more service in God's glory; then the Great Fire of 1666, which destroyed two-thirds of London, including Milton's last piece of real estate. To get money he was forced to sell his books and publish anything, such as *The Art of Logic* written in his youth, that would pass the censor. In 1667, he earned some needed money from the publication of *Paradise Lost* (in ten books, later expanded to twelve). It was the only volume of his poetry to sell, and he was at last recognized as a poet rather than as the propagandist hated by many of his countrymen. Before completing (or revising) *Samson Agonistes,* he composed a "brief epic" about Christ's temptations by Satan, *Paradise Regained,* another work reflecting Milton's lifelong devotion to reading, especially the Bible. Several additional works were posthumously published: a *History of Britain,* begun in

1649 and never finished, and *A Brief History of Moscovia* (published in 1682) that reveals his interest in geography and history.

Alone with his third wife in his final years, Milton lived in quiet retirement. He suffered from gout and arthritis but cheerfully greeted the many visitors who came to call on the famous old poet who had witnessed and written so much in a revolutionary time. We read of his being "generous in relieving the wants of his friends," despite his own limited means, and of being "merry." Not a tragic or defeated old man, he continued to fight with amazing vitality, as his pamphlet, *Of True Religion* (1673) attests, and found in poetry a vehicle for expressing many of the doubts and conflicts that had racked him as a propagandist. His last days were serene perhaps because he saw his life's ambitions fulfilled and could foresee the acclaim that would come after he was gone. Milton died peacefully on November 8, 1674, a month short of his sixty-sixth birthday. An elaborate funeral, attended by John Dryden and Andrew Marvell among many other distinguished men, was held at the London church of St. Giles, Cripplegate, where he was buried beside his father.

If Milton and his poetry have the power to move us today, it is in part because his life and work are inseparable; each of his works is stamped with his strong personality and commitment to ideas. He remains remarkable for the constancy and courage he exhibited amid shifting poetic fashions and amid personal and public turbulence. His life ended, the enormous influence of his work on world literature was about to be felt.

# 2

# "The Lofty Rhyme": The Early Poems, *Comus*, and "Lycidas"

The early poems of Milton are important in anticipating his later achievement as well as indicating the extent of his youthful mastery of English, Latin, and Italian verse forms. Many of these minor poems, belonging to the first thirty years of his life, would be "major" in the canon of a lesser poet. Some are largely experiments or exercises, others are more inspired in form and feeling, but all reveal a singular independence, Milton standing apart from the prevailing "schools" of seventeenth-century verse. Although he owes more to the influence of Edmund Spenser than to any other poet, Milton tends to be more classical and European than his English contemporaries; even as a young poet, he also seems more serious and ambitious. With his confidence and patriotism, he shares in none of the pessimism found in much Jacobean writing. He is more old-fashioned in style than Donne, more religious and idealistic than Jonson, and he anticipates the public tone and rational optimism associated with the age of Dryden and Pope. Milton wrote some of the most beautiful short poems in the language but regarded them "as no more than preparations for his real task, his ultimate ambition, which was to write a lofty and elaborate poem."[1] Of major interest to today's readers of these early works is witnessing the creative process of a gifted, experimental poet. Although many of them are occasional, prompted by specific personal or public situations, they reveal the poet's preparation for his literary career. Features of the later poems are found in these early works, including his feel for language and his skill in creating elaborate verse paragraphs and long sentences that were to become the hallmark of his style.

One remarkable aspect of Milton's early poems is that many are in Latin. The use of Latin (and Italian) was in part a snobbish pose, a sign of independence, a repudiation of his own society; it was sometimes a means of dealing with erotic or bawdy topics; it was also a standard medium for a scholarly young man, steeped in the classics, who had ambitions that extended beyond his own country and who felt that English was inadequate for these lofty purposes. Thus, when, at age nineteen, he speaks to his fellow Cambridge students in the "Vacation Exercise," part of his sixth Latin Prolusion, or mock oration, it is both surprising and daring that he should use the vernacular and express (with "Hail native Language") his enthusiasm for English and his intention to put it to worthy purposes. He uses the academic exercise to reveal his view of poetry as noble and moral. Elements of the later Miltonic voice and aspiration are clear as he shows his allegiance to the old Spenserian style of the Elizabethans rather than to that of his fashionable metaphysical contemporaries. This 1628 poem in heroic couplets provides a stiff but revealing look at the earnest young poet certain of his ability to impress his audience.

In the same year Milton composed an elegy in rhyme royal, "On the Death of a Fair Infant Dying of a Cough," prompted by the death of the daughter of his sister Anne. It is an ambitious work full of rhetorical questions, Spenserian archaisms ("Whilom," "eld"), and conceits very different from those used by the metaphysical poets. Unlike the more successful Nativity Ode, with which it is often compared, the "Fair Infant" tries but does not succeed in using classical allusions effectively to treat the theme of untimely death. In the fifth stanza Milton eloquently states the theme of immortality but seems uncertain about the "something" divine in the child's face and about the way to express the reality of sudden, accidental death. He seems unsure, too, about the suitability of Ovidian imagery—the personified winter (death) and Apollo (the sun)—to express Christian consolation. The questions that follow, addressed to the child's soul, do not resolve the issue of premature death and indicate a largely Platonic view. In the ninth stanza, the contrived questions and doubts lead to a Christian conclusion: the infant's soul is an angel, a heavenly messenger who can intercede for those on earth faced with sin and "pestilence." At the end the poem shifts suddenly to a consolation in the form of a moralistic address to the child's mother.

Despite its weaknesses, the poem looks forward to Milton's later work because of his use of classical allusions to give weight and solemnity to his sister's loss and his contrasting images and shifting use of color, light, and dark. While striving for the formal, learned, impersonal tone of the traditional elegy, the poet tries to combine classical form and imagery with Christian meaning, showing the superiority of the latter. The initial conceit of the flower that tempted winter to kiss it is striking but becomes strained because of the elaborate mythology. The elegy is clearly an exercise by a young poet emotionally and technically unsure of himself. Some of the lines have the typical Miltonic flavor—serious, eloquent, learned, Latinate, musical—but the question and answer, the repeated shifting from classical to Christian and back again, and the anticlimactic ending show that he has not succeeded either in integrating classical and Christian material or in confronting the reality of death in a deeply felt way. The poem reveals Milton's reluctance to involve his experience and emotion.[2] In contrast to "Lycidas," in which the poet shows himself capable of maturely expressing sincere feelings, the "Fair Infant" reflects his interest in his own poetic artifice rather than the issues of loss, grief, and consolation.

Milton's first major poem, composed at Christmas 1629, celebrates the mystery of the Incarnation. As such, "On the Morning of Christ's Nativity," usually called the Nativity Ode, is more than a poem on the Nativity alone. By a subtle mixture of images of light and sound and of classical and Christian allusions, Milton beautifully develops a picture of universal peace in which darkness is lighted, harmony retuned, and nature transcended because the Son of God has become man. One of the great achievements of the poem is Milton's ability to use light (representing divine love, wisdom, and power) in such a way that the conquest of the dark by the light becomes metaphorically inseparable from the establishment of universal musical harmony. The picture of the Christmas stable is expressed as a sacred song.

We begin in a timeless present when the historical birth of Christ, the Christmas of 1629, and all Christmases are contemporaneous. We are then given a picture of the silent night of the Nativity when fallen nature was restored by the "Prince of

Light," whose reign of peace leads to a revival of man's lost capacity for perfection, conveyed in terms of the legendary music of the spheres, and to a prophecy of perfect harmony at the end of time. After the proem, the thematic frame through which we view the ode itself, the Hymn or song of celebration begins with a picture of nature expectantly awaiting the peaceful birth (stanzas 1–8), followed by a treatment of concord or musical harmony (9 through 18) and the conquest of the discord of paganism by the light of Christ (19 through 26) before the conclusion returns to the Christmas stable. The dramatic contrasts—between past and present, sound and silence, light and dark, music and discord—constitute a powerful mingling of aural and visual images that convey a sense of wonder akin to that produced by Baroque art. For the poem describes a picture and an event calculated to astonish the reader with a dramatization of Christ's power throughout history. The temporal movement in the ode, along with its use of imperatives (stanza 4), oxymoronic surprise (line 3), immediacy, and paradox, also contributes to the Baroque feeling. This effect reflects Milton's belief that perfection is not a condition of stasis, for man is not ideally at rest but in action and in motion, as expressed by the poem's predominantly musical imagery.

The proem, in four rhyme royal stanzas, captures at once the temporal paradox of the birth of the "Son of Heav'n's eternal King." The past event of the first Christmas is made simultaneously equivalent with every Christmas to express the timeless mystery that Christ was, and is, an infant who must die just as he has died for "Our great redemption." The tenses therefore shift from the insistent immediacy of the present in the opening line to the past (4), then to the future (6). Needing aid to express the great Christian mystery, the poet asks for the gift of a song or poem that he might present to the "Infant God": this gift is the Hymn itself, the ode or formal song of celebration that develops the theme indicated in the proem. With a sense of urgency, the speaker's present imperatives ("See," "run") with their visual immediacy reinforce the sense of the timeless present.

The Hymn, in which Milton uses an original eight-line stanza form, is more ornate and classical than the introduction; it celebrates the effect of the Incarnation on human time. Just as the Son has "laid aside" (12) his divinity, nature has put aside her power in deference to the Child, who now "lies" in the manger. Mother earth is imagined as rejecting "the sun, her lusty Paramour" (36), who is less worthy than the true bridegroom, Christ. Since nature was weakened because of the Fall, she is seen as "guilty" and in need of purification. She is also aware of her inferiority to Christ's peace, which, dovelike, softly descends in a lovely, fluid, Baroque movement, suggested by the participles (47, 48, 50, 51), to bring heavenly harmony to earth (a reference to the Roman world at peace for seven years before Christ's birth). The frozen "picture" of suspenseful silence (stanza 4) is followed by a hushed sense (line 64) of nature awaiting Christ's coming. Ovid's halcyons either suggest God's Spirit creating the world or the Holy Spirit appearing as a dove at Christ's baptism; the "Birds of Calm" (68) express the beginning of Christ's kingdom by the typically Miltonic technique of multiple allusion. So, too, "Lucifer" (74) signifies either the morning star or the sun, but the overtones of Satan's heavenly name inevitably remind us also of Christ's adversary in the conflict between good and evil. The sun has been put to shame by the "greater Sun" of the Son of God, a conventional play on words that allows for a comparison between the powerful light of Christ and that of the weakened sun god, Apollo. The poet then provides a brief glimpse of the shepherds viewing the spectacular event; they see in Pan a pre-Christian prefiguring of Christ the Good Shepherd.

After the emphasis shifts from light (and darkness) to sound, the conquest of darkness by light in stanzas 9 through 18 becomes coterminous with the restoration of heavenly music. The Platonic music of the spheres (line 98) is used to suggest universal peace and perfection, as proclaimed by angelic hosts "in glittering ranks" (114), an image fusing light and sound as the earth is serenaded by the other spheres. Christ is not only the light of the world but also the ruler of the planets, whose perfect turning reveals God's orderly plan of creation. In stanza 13 the poet alludes to the golden age promised in Virgil's *Eclogue IV*, traditionally interpreted as prophesying the coming of the Messiah, and to Plato's cyclical "Great Year" (*Timaeus*, 39), along with the Pythagorean tradition that the music of the spheres was audible to sinless man.[3] Having called for this celestial harmony, the speaker, imagining that Christ's reign of peace has been established on earth, recognizes that his ecstatic vision is premature: earthly perfection must await the conflict between good and evil that is to be waged as history runs its course. The Incarnation has occurred because of the Redemption; Bethlehem leads to Calvary, as is clear from stanza 16, in which the Babe's timeless present coexists with his future action "on the bitter cross." The speaker recognizes, too, that Judgment Day must occur before true heavenly harmonies can be heard on earth. The final defeat of Satan by the Redeemer begins, the speaker tells us, on "this happy day" (line 167) and leads to the traditional procession of the false gods, whose reign comes to an end with the birth of Christ. Milton the humanist, rather than condemning the pagan gods of classical antiquity, pities them, as his tone of lament (stanza 20) indicates. The terror of the horrific gods counterpoints the beauty and joy of the rest of the poem. In his list of Roman, Phoenician, and Egyptian deities, analogous to the epic catalog in Book 2 of *Paradise Lost,* Milton shows more animosity toward the false gods of ancient Palestine, such as Dagon, who were opposed by the Israelites, than for the Graeco-Roman deities. Osiris (line 213), a pagan judge of the dead, is meant to contrast with Christ the Judge at the end of time; the Egyptian deity feels (stanza 25) the power of the brilliant light of the newborn Child, who reveals his power even in his infancy. So, too, the infant Hercules, who strangled the serpents sent by jealous Hera to kill him, is alluded to as a type of Christ (line 228) in contrast with the Satanic figure of Typhon, who is either the huge serpent thrown down from Olympus or the evil Egyptian deity who slayed Osiris. Again Milton attempts to integrate what he saw as false classical lore with Christian truths.

The final stanza returns us to the sense of astonishment with which we began. The conceit of the "Sun in bed" banishing night as the Son with his creative power banishes the darkness of the pagan gods recalls a similar conceit at 79–80 and prepares for the quiet simplicity of the Nativity scene, which contrasts with the spectacular clashes of light and dark, discord and harmony now ended. The sun is no longer Christ's rival but his deputy; its daily rising reflects the cyclical triumph of good over evil that coexists in the poem with the linear progression of history, Milton emphasizing that the birth of Christ is both timeless and historical. With the Mother and Child surrounded by bright angels, love, expressed as light, dispels darkness and brings order, stability, and peace.

The Nativity Ode is a remarkable achievement for a poet of twenty-one. Its sweeping temporal-historical scope ranges from the beginning to the end of time while expressing the timeless omnipresence of the divine Birth. It is typically Miltonic in being independent of others' styles, combining classical dignity with joyous feeling and achieving originality by handling traditional ideas in new ways. Although he would soon discard the Spenserian archaisms and pictorial conceits, Milton is able to suggest the direction of his later style, with its mastery of sound, its universal scope, and its use of pagan allusion to reinforce Christian ideas.

Milton's poem on Shakespeare, published in the second folio of 1632, reflects the prevailing view of the dramatist as a spontaneous genius, a child of nature who, in "L'Allegro," warbles "his native Woodnotes wild," in contrast to more learned poets such as Ben Jonson. Of special significance is Milton's conceit of Shakespeare's "livelong Monument," suggesting that his readers' "admiration of him transforms each one of them into a likeness of a marble statue, within which, as in a marble tomb his lines are buried."[4] Milton, expanding the conventional Petrarchan idea that admiration transforms the beholder into the likeness of a statue, is less concerned with Shakespeare than with a strikingly original image about the permanence of literary fame. As J. B. Leishman observes, such ingenuity is typical of many seventeenth-century eulogies and funeral elegies.[5] Whether the poet evinces any genuine admiration for Shakespeare remains a critical issue. By addressing the bulk of the poem to Shakespeare as if he were still alive, Milton emphasizes the permanent value of the great poet's work. And he pays subtle homage to him by alluding in the final line to the last line of Shakespeare's Sonnet 29 ("That then I scorn to change my state with kings") to suggest that even kings would forego life to be enshrined in Shakespeare's immortal monument.

"On Time" and "At a Solemn Music" owe something to Shakespeare in language and to Spenser and the madrigal in form and stately pace. Both concern the contrast between earthly flux and heavenly stability, between Platonic and Christian idealism. In the first poem, the apostrophe to personified time and the duality of matter and spirit are conventional, yet the speaker's challenge to time is also an effective means for him to reassert his faith in God and his hope of seeing the beatific vision (the "happy-making sight") resulting from the "individual" (everlasting) kiss when eternity greets each person. "At a Solemn Music" is a meditation on spiritual harmony and its power to revive dead things; it concerns the ideal of poetry and music as sister arts that jointly penetrate the soul. As in "Il Penseroso," the Lydian mode is seen as causing the soul of the singer to meet that of the hearer. To this Milton adds the fanciful hope that the reader, like unfallen Adam or Eve, might hear the "fair music" of the universe, which is conceived as a mighty instrument.

"L'Allegro" and "Il Penseroso," probably written in 1631, are among Milton's most appealing poems, often praised as the most flawless examples of his youthful art. They exemplify two contrasting and complementary moods, those of the genial and of the pensive man. The first speaker is cheerful, the second melancholy in the classical sense of serious and thoughtful. Clearly, the black melancholy of depression dismissed in the opening of the first poem is not the contemplation invoked in the second. The pursuits of both speakers are pursuits of delight and reflection. Milton, although identifying himself with both personae, has been accused of making the mirthful and meditative men too much alike or of clearly siding with the latter. But the poems are meant to be imagined as two halves of one whole, or as their titles imply, contrasting movements in a musical composition; they are companion pieces, "a type popular in a period when people were fond of companion pictures."[6] Although Milton's temperament would suggest more affinity with the solitary, spiritual joys of Penseroso than with Allegro's more social pleasures, one cannot conclude that one poem reflects a truer vision of happiness or that it represents the poet's preference. In fact, the balanced view of life described in the poems suggests that neither approach by itself can be satisfying; the first poem shows what pleasures and activities will correct the "divinest Melancholy" of the second. Rosemond Tuve, seeing the works as encomiums, or poems of praise, finds that they express the direct, simple relation between lived and imagined experiences "typifying what is universally pleasurable and universally desired."[7] Like conventional contrasts between Youth and Age, Comedy and Tragedy, or Action and Contemplation in the tradition of academic debate to which they are indirectly related, the two poems are idealized portraits of two alternative attitudes toward life.

The parallels in these formal, symmetrically conceived works begin at once with the witty dismissal of the other side, expressed with hyperbole and Ovidian allusion, intended to startle and impress the reader. There follows an invocation to a goddess to establish the mood, specific parallels (such as the companions Liberty and Contemplation), and a generalized itinerary of day or night in which pleasures are initiated by the song of a bird (lark and nightingale). From the sounds of morning and evening, respectively, the poet progresses to pictorial, pastoral scenes, then moves from country to city before the happiness provided by music is invoked. In "L'Allegro," the Lydian airs provide a rapture so intense, the speaker says, that it would have led Orpheus to free Eurydice from death completely; in "Il Penseroso," it leads appropriately to religious ecstasy. This second poem ends in the morning when its companion piece began, indicating a cyclical completion. The longer treatment of melancholy is in keeping with the more thoughtful pace of the contemplative man.

Among the many contrasts, Allegro's pleasures usually involve human society; when alone, he is taken out of himself by what he sees, whereas the pleasures of Il Penseroso are more introspective and solitary. The only sign of human society in his meditation comes from the organ music, which leads to images of spiritual harmony. Apparently sleeping by day, the second speaker begins his night by strolling alone in a dark wood, listening to a nightingale, and gazing at the moon. He prolongs his reverie further by sitting alone by the fire, then by retiring to "some high lonely Tow'r" to read, rather than watch, a Greek tragedy (unlike his counterpart who enjoys English comedy). The result, however, is not grim or funereal, just as mirth is not seen as jolly or hilarious so much as lighthearted. "One poem is the other in reverse, in time sequence, the succession of light and shadow, of sounds. One is a poem of cheerful, shrill sounds and of light; the other of muted sounds and shadows."[8]

Responding to T. S. Eliot's complaint that the poems are too "general" in imagery, Leishman among others shows that Milton did not set out to provide detailed pictures of natural scenes or objects but instead precisely evokes the pleasures appropriate to two contrasted moods.[9] The poet gives us a nonparticularized setting; since the subject is everyone's mirth or melancholy, his suggestive poetry allows us to imagine the details. The pastoral imagery allows us in "L'Allegro" to savor the nature or essence of joy when it is free of the cares that limit real experience.[10] In keeping with the decorum of the poems, the imagery, then, properly reflects the universal subject. The octosyllabic couplet, popularized by various Elizabethan and Jacobean poets, is ideally suited to Milton's subject and tone. The metrical dexterity of the poems as well as their smooth verbal skills, their freshness, simplicity, and immediacy of description, have long delighted readers and disarmed critics. Archie Burnett notes that Milton's language produces an impressionistic style, especially in lines 147–50 of "Il Penseroso," where alliteration, assonance, rhyme, and "ambiguously floating syntax" convey the mystery of a dream.[11] The poems suggest an indebtedness to several English poets, especially to the Shakespeare of *A Midsummer Night's Dream.* Along with the other early poems, they reveal the development of Milton's own voice, showing that his originality consists in large part of developing in a more precise and striking way what other poets had created.

Milton composed his first major poems, a masque and an elegy, before his Italian journey; they reflect his intensive period of scholarly study after he left Cambridge. Each is a remarkable achievement in which the young poet, using the pastoral mode, reveals his ability to transcend the occasional nature of a work and to redefine its genre.

*A Mask Presented at Ludlow Castle* was Milton's name for the work popularly known as *Comus,* a misleading title since the evil seducer Comus is no more the hero of the masque than Satan is the hero of *Paradise Lost.* Its theme, the triumph of virtue over vice, was typical of court masques, yet as usual with Milton his only full-length masque is more complex and philosophical than works by other authors in this genre. Henry Lawes, with whom Milton had worked on *Arcades,* an earlier, shorter masque than *Comus,* was the composer and stage manager for the production, which was performed on September 29, 1634. The Lady was played by fifteen-year-old Lady Alice Egerton; the Elder Brother by eleven-year-old Lord Brackley; and the Second Brother by Thomas Egerton, age nine; all had some experience as masque performers. Lawes played the attendant Spirit.

*Comus* is one of the last English masques. These were indoor entertainments involving music, spectacle, and disguised dancers, who interacted with the spectators, and were presented by amateurs usually to honor royalty or nobility. The collaboration of Ben Jonson and the designer-architect Inigo Jones early in the seventeenth century, and the taste of the Jacobean court, had transformed these aristocratic masquerades into elegant entertainments featuring romantic music and mythological, pastoral poetry, with a text based on some classical subject. The dialogue and theme were secondary to dance and spectacle, which was enhanced by elaborate stage machinery. The result was not naturalistic drama but an operalike pageant. The main masque plot was combined with antimasque revelry, represented in Milton's work by Comus and his unruly followers. Despite its music and staging, *Comus* is sometimes seen more as a poem than as a true masque. Though probably less extravagant in costume and spectacle than most court masques, it is certainly more serious, with extensive dialogue and a minimum of dance and pageantry. Yet it remains in the masque tradition, using a simple fable and a pastoral setting, along with magic, allegory, and music, to honor a specific occasion (the inauguration of the Earl of Bridgewater as Lord President of Wales) and to compliment the noble audience, which joins with the masquers in the final dance of celebration. And, in the spirit of Jonson's masques, with their emphasis on poetry and moral idealism, the Christian theme is expressed in conventionally Platonic terms. Accordingly, Milton transforms his masque into a beautiful poetic vehicle for serious moral philosophy, so that *Comus* has a permanent literary value that the typical masque lacks.

In the opening lines, the Spirit introduces the masque's prevailing Platonic cast of thought by contrasting spirit and matter. His heavenly abode exists in opposition to the "dim spot" of earth where men benighted by sinfulness may be unaware of "the crown that Virtue gives" to "her true Servants," such as the Lady, the principal character of the work. The Spirit proceeds to praise England and "this tract" (Wales), where a "noble Peer" (the Earl of Bridgewater) and his three children will enact an allegorical journey through an ominous wood. The Spirit has thus set the scene: the young actors will present a lofty entertainment to celebrate their father's "new-entrusted Scepter." The Spirit, who is to be a pastoral guide, has been sent, like a guardian angel, to defend the young Lady. It is no surprise that some beast or villain lurks in the dark forest.

As we are told about Comus, the son of Bacchus and Circe, we see Milton's original development of the Circe myth (from the *Odyssey,* book 10). It forms a central part of the fairy-tale plot in which the imprisoning charms of an evil magician are undone by the action of a good magician, Sabrina, whose cool, watery presence will contrast with the heated intoxication of the son of Bacchus, god of wine. As son of Circe, Comus turns people into beasts by "Off'ring to every weary Traveller / His orient liquor in a Crystal Glass" (64–65). Like the enchantress Acrasia in *The Faerie Queene* (2.12), a Circelike figure of intemperance, Comus offers the false light of his shining liquid rather than the true light of virtue. Comus's magic transforms only the faces, not the entire bodies, of his victims, thus degrading the image of God in man. The pagan-classical elements in the work typically point to a Christian moral: The dark wood of error and deceit represents the treacherous worldly testing ground through which every Christian must pass on his earthly sojourn as he confronts temptation.

In typical antimasque style, Comus and his crew, a "rout of Monsters," enter, making a "riotous and unruly noise" that contrasts with the dancelike rhythms of his speech. His Platonic language ("We that are of purer fire / Imitate the Starry Choir") is as false as his dance (the "measure" that begins at line 145), which is not the usual sign of harmony and order nor of the spontaneity that true virtue brings; the monsters are enslaved, acting only on command, a parody of virtue's authentic freedom. It is also ironic that the language of pastoral innocence (115–21) is used by an evil seducer. Though his appeal to Venus is one of the work's few erotic overtones (downplayed because of youthful performers), the emphasis on temptation in *Comus,* Milton's first work on this crucial theme in his poetry, looks ahead to the speeches of Satan to Eve in *Paradise Lost.* Comus is self-deceived, trapped by his own illogic, and so is morally enslaved to a greater degree than the Lady will be. He often speaks in images of "snares," traps, and tangles (161–65) and quickly assumes a pastoral disguise when the Lady enters.

Lost in "the blind mazes of this tangl'd Wood," the Lady speaks with lofty contempt for the riotous sounds of merrymakers, scorning the rustic crudity of a pastoral world she will soon trust. Her two brothers, it is learned, have left her to seek some cooling fruit to relieve her thirst. Though alone in the dark forest, she is not terrified but wonders where her brothers are and why the night cannot light her way. She is apprehensive only because her natural virtue and reason might be corrupted. As she begins to entertain fearful fantasies, she reassures herself that the virtuous mind cannot be assaulted. Calling upon Faith, Hope, and the "unblemish't form of Chastity," she is comforted by God ("the Supreme good") and sees "a sable cloud / Turn forth her silver lining on the night" (221–22). Her recollection of the virtues brings a heavenly light, even in the darkest of places. Because of her virtue, the darkness cannot vitiate the Lady's innocent nature. At the same time, she develops an awareness of virtue and light as well as of their opposites.

Her sweet, airy song to Echo does not summon her brothers; rather Comus, the figure of Misrule, ironically appears accompanied by wild noise and jazzy rhythms. As with Satan's first glimpse of Adam and Eve, the seducer is overwhelmed by the Lady's virtuous beauty, which he sees in terms of musical "ravishment." The virtue-vice polarity had thus been established not only by images of light and darkness, and harmony and discord; for Comus, the evil counterpart of Orpheus, has inherited his mother's gift for music. After an aside (244–66), the disguised seducer addresses her as a "foreign wonder," pointing up the opposition between the central characters and the separate worlds they inhabit. After a formal exchange, she accepts the "harmless" villager's offer to accompany him to a safe cottage. Though acknowledging Comus's fulsome praise (271), the Lady nevertheless comes to trust the honest, simple courtesy of the shepherd, which is seen as preferable to the "tap'stry Halls" of princes (reminding us of Ludlow Castle itself, transformed into a forest for the occasion). He pretends that reuniting her with her brothers will be "a journey like the path to Heaven," inverting the essential nature of the allegorical journey, which the Lady rightly terms a "trial" or test of virtue (329), though she is innocently unaware that she is being led to a hellish place of sinful enslavement.

As soon as Comus and the Lady leave the scene, the two brothers appear, asking the moon to provide them with a "rule of streaming light" (340), *rule* also referring to reason. When the young brother worries about his lost sister, the Elder Brother never swerves from his stoic conviction that their sister is protected by her innate virtue with its "radiant light" (374). Like the speaker of "Il Penseroso," he talks of "sweet retired Solitude," yet the younger brother remains afraid until he hears his elder's philosophical discourse on the "hidden strength" of heavenly chastity that clads their sister "in complete steel." The speech (418–75) resembles an academic lecture, supported by classical authorities, asserting that the "true virginity" of chastity will save her. Appeals to classical sources are followed by a more Christianized discussion of "Saintly chastity" that contrasts carnal sensuality with the "unpolluted temple of the mind," indicating the key Miltonic theme of free will: One cannot be morally hurt except by yielding to passions.

The Elder Brother's speech on virtue reminds one of the value in being strong-minded and living a life that is the outward manifestation of an inner philosophy. On a strictly natural level, he is correct; his sister has nothing to fear, but on the supernatural level, he is shortsighted: One needs outside aid (grace); the virtuous Lady cannot save herself.

The Spirit, disguised as the shepherd Thyrsis, in contrast to Comus's deceptively rustic pose, interrupts the discussion; his speech (513–79) with its lush imagery indirectly dramatizes the brothers' fear and grief in a way that their own speeches do not. We hear again of the contrast between the "barbarous dissonance" of Comus and the contemplative repose associated with nature; and the Lady's virtue is associated with the harmonious sound that "Rose like a stream of rich distill'd Perfumes, / And Stole upon the Air" (556–57). The Spirit has taken the form of a shepherd talented at playing music, a skill that would remind the classically educated listeners of Orpheus, whose playing could draw the best and most generous qualities from animals and gods, again in contrast to Comus, whose music degrades his followers. The imagined picture of the Lady in the grip of the "damn'd wizard" causes the younger brother again to proclaim his fear, requiring his older brother to offer another lecture on the power of virtue ("Virtue may be assail'd but never hurt") before they prepare to rescue her. Thyrsis advises them that physical force will be useless in overcoming the sorcerer but that Haemony, a magical plant, like the special root that Hermes gives Odysseus as a safeguard, will enable them to assault the wizard's hall. The brothers are told to charge at Comus with swords drawn, to break his glass, and seize his magic wand.

Meanwhile, in the masque's climactic scene, the Lady sits immobilized in Comus's "enchanted Chair." Her first speech ("Fool, do not boast, / Thou canst not touch the freedom of my mind / With all thy charms") indicates that her virtuous nature transcends the blandishments of her tempter. The result is a confrontation or stylized debate, rather than a genuine dramatic conflict, since she is able to penetrate his arguments and thus to resist temptation. Their exchange would be familiar to that of educated people of the time since its theme is nature as the source of norms for self-government: Does nature teach one to indulge or to restrain oneself? As the Epicurean spokesman for the *carpe diem* position, Comus urges the Lady to seize the moment and live for now. As Satan will insinuate to Eve, Comus says that to refrain from enjoying nature is perverse. (The appeals are mostly to hunger and thirst, but lines 679–81 suggest a sexual temptation as well.) In his most important speech (706–55) Comus equates chastity with abstinence, presenting a false view of liberty whereby those who are wanton are seen as truly disciplined; thus he argues that temperance is unnatural ("Th'all-giver would be unthank't"). In poetically and rhetorically skillful language, he urges her to enjoy nature ("Beauty is nature's coin, must not be hoarded") and reveals his own moral disorder by confusing liberty with license. The Lady, perceiving the false arguments of the seducer from the outset, cannot reason with an evil force in what she calls "unhallow'd air." Unlike Eve, who listens to and engages the serpent in dialogue, the Lady has a moral strength and lofty philosophy that render her virtue not susceptible to temptation: "Impostor, do not charge most innocent nature." Then she questions the purpose of a debate with one who "dares" to speak "Against the Sun-clad power of Chastity"; as she says, he is not "fit" to be persuaded that nature must be controlled and temperately used. She is aware of the threat of her tempter yet is capable of indignantly rejecting him. Perhaps she fears that she will lose her emotional control if she tries to deal with such an irrational force. When it is felt that the debate could go on indefinitely, the brothers rush in but let the seducer escape with his wand; thus the Lady remains passively "fixt" in her chair, in need of special external aid. Haemony, like reason, is unable to subdue a supernatural force. The Spirit will call upon Sabrina, a "Virgin pure" who is goddess of the nearby Severn River. A typical masque nymph, she combines natural and supernatural qualities since she has been bathed in spiritual waters "with Asphodel" (Homer's flower of immortality) and so can be seen as a figure of grace. She represents the permanent freedom of virtue needed to release the Lady from the enslaving power of the sorcerer. The song ("Sabrina fair") with its imagery of light and water depicts the goddess sitting freely "under the glassy, cool, translucent wave," in contrast to the constrained sitting of the Lady, whose passive, natural virtue requires active, supernatural aid. The "loose train" of Sabrina's hair also suggests the freedom of virtue ("Love virtue, she alone is free") that is Milton's central theme.

The Song causes the Lady to rise, and soon she will be sprinkled with drops of Sabrina's heavenly power. With the Lady's rescue, the Spirit urges her and her brothers to flee to their father's nearby residence. In true masque style, the young actors step forth to dance with the assembled guests in Ludlow Castle, but Milton, making sure that his work instructs as well as entertains, adds a moral epilogue in which the Spirit emphasizes the Youth and Joy that come to those who have virtue and that are the true result of the self-control Comus had scorned. As the conclusion makes clear, freedom only comes from love of virtue. A "crown of deathless praise" is the heavenly reward for those who successfully withstand what Milton in the *Christian Doctrine* called the "good temptation" whereby God tests man's faith or patience (James 1.12).

Milton has adapted the masque genre to emphasize his central theme of choice, for freedom rather than chastity is at the heart of *Comus*. Instead of relying on a sudden revelation, metamorphosis, or solved riddle, as in the typical masque, Milton uses the genre to express a serious theme involving the contrasts among the natural, unnatural, and supernatural. The radiant light of virtue, the poem's main image, reveals the theme that the Platonic inner life keeps the soul free to choose virtuous action. Despite the Lady's initial blindness to Comus's real character, the darkness cannot deny her essential innocence, and her virtuous light shines ever bright. But since she can be tricked by the seducer's external charms, one sees that light on the natural level, while signifying reason or wisdom, is not bright enough to help her fully penetrate Comus's evil or to save her from the consequences of his blindness. As the son of Circe ("the daughter of the sun"), Comus is the grandson of the source of physical light; but Sabrina, associated with water and light, is both a force of nature and an agent of grace. This goddess of the river can liberate the enslaved Lady, who must progress from passive to active, natural to supernatural, virtue. Thus the central action of the masque—the overthrow of one magician by another—reveals, as in Shakespeare's *The Tempest,* that magic can result in enslavement or be the means of liberation and that adhering to the norms of Nature, a manifestation of self-control, will become supernatural virtue when validated by grace. The power of the language to suggest related images of light, freedom, and harmony is a remarkable achievement in which Milton makes the conflict clear, not simply by action but also by contrasting images.

Yet Milton is not content with a simple light-dark dichotomy, as Comus's false light and the "Benighted" Lady indicate.[12] The poem does not merely equate natural darkness with evil and goodness with light; as Comus himself says, " 'Tis only daylight that makes Sin" (126). Her "sable cloud" with its "silver lining" brightens the unnaturally "drear" wood and helps her to see what virtue is. Her recalling the heavenly virtues enables her vision to develop, and divine light guides those who can find it and live by it. The dark wood, as in Dante and Spenser, represents the threat of temptation and evil; it is also a rural setting where the fantastic can occur. Renaissance pastoral poetry typically expresses a tension between rural simplicity and rural grossness.[13] As such, the Lady associates the evil of Comus with the crudity of peasants before acknowledging (in lines 320–24) the elements of natural goodness and simplicity, typical of country life, that lead her to follow the shepherd-seducer.

Such a setting is apt for the conflict between nature (the arguments of Comus) and grace (the strength that protects the Lady). Her spirituality is incomplete, requiring Sabrina's liberation, which reveals that nature is on the side of virtue in the conflict with Comus. He, posing as nature's champion, condemns discipline as unnatural; Sabrina reveals that nature and grace interact, resulting in the freedom of authentic virtue. Although Comus, like Satan, seems persuasive in his arguments, his rhetoric and sophistical reasoning are deceptive. Giving the best poetry to villains such as Comus does not mean that the poet is on their side—indeed his clear conviction is that the good will always triumph—but that vice can appear more attractive than virtue. Comus has argued that one's appetites are inherently licit, creating for the Lady a paradise that panders to every desire. With her reason and natural virtue, however, the Lady can distinguish between overindulgence and temperance. Although she cannot penetrate the "harmless villager" disguise of Comus, she can detect the sophistry of his temptation, finally refuting his attempt to ensnare her mind.

The poem conceives of the "sun-clad" power of chastity metaphorically. It is not abstinence, as Comus insists, but a positive good, a purity of life, seen as the key virtue by Platonists, who considered all virtues as self-purifying. According to the reading of Plato by the Renaissance philosopher Marsilio Ficino, chastity means a consecration of the soul to the good. Milton shows that chastity is not a negative virtue, a denial, but a "disposition to love,"[14] a spiritual wholesomeness enabling one to control passion with reason and grace. It involves self-discipline. To be chaste is to be clad in spiritual armor, seeing all things by the steady light of virtue.[15] Although the poet's language is philosophical rather than theological, the religious implications of the masque are made clear, especially by the attendant Spirit, who points beyond "Jove's Court" to the Christian Heaven. His epilogue reflects Milton's view of discipline, as stated in *The Reason of Church Government:* it is the basis of the free expression of creative energy. Through discipline, virtue becomes "audible to mortal ears" and freedom is discovered in the total commitment to virtue.[16]

The Spirit, having descended from the celestial to the earthly realm, is central to the vertical-horizontal pattern of the ideas and action. And he says that whoever tasted Comus's cup "lost his upright shape, / And downward fell" (52–53) from rationality into bestiality. "The masque reflects man's central position on the Great Chain of Being, confronted with the way up into being or the way down into self-annihilation."[17] Sabrina rises to assist the Lady rise from the enchanted chair, freeing her from the power of Comus. He leads down, destroying the image of God in men by transforming their faces into "some brutish form" (70). The divine reflection in the individual is associated with the gift of reason (525–29), as in *Paradise Lost* 4.288–94. Roger Wilkenfeld finds that Milton's plot is composed of two movements: a horizontal or linear movement of the Lady and her brothers through the wood to the safety of their home and a vertical movement that explores "symbolically the central theme . . . the nature of freedom."[18] According to this interpretation, the immobilized Lady is at the center of a series of vertical and horizontal movements that capture the elegance of Milton's ideas and masque structure. The descent of the Spirit, the ascent and descent of Sabrina, and the ascent of the Lady and the Spirit at the end symbolize the movement from earthly disharmony and discord to heavenly harmony and order. When the freely moving Sabrina faces the restrained Lady, there is the climactic metaphoric expression of the relationship between freedom and restraint in contrast to the constrained, forced dance of Comus and his crew. The lost Lady (lost virtue) can only be restored by spiritual purification and discipline, by an effort to rise above the fallen world of sensuality. Comus and his followers point the way down to bestiality, whereas Sabrina points the way up through grace to true virtue. The epilogue reminds the reader of Milton's central moral ideas: Virtue is the source of freedom, whereas sin enslaves; the way to virtue is by discipline, but the way to Heaven is by virtue and grace.

Four years after the completion of *Comus*, "Lycidas" was published in a 1638 collection of elegies by Cambridge friends of Edward King, who had drowned the year before. "Lycidas," which Milton called a monody or personal lament, is a pastoral elegy in which the death of one man is universalized in terms of art, nature, rebirth, order, and compassion. From the outset, Milton's concern with broader issues—the death of poetic inspiration along with themes of love, immortality, friendship, and renewal—is apparent. Reading this intricate, richly allusive poem, like listening to a variety of intermingled melodies, is to encounter what many critics have called the most powerful statement in English poetry of the acceptance of what seems unacceptable.[19] Traditional yet innovative and personal, it is the most significant of Milton's short poems and is often considered not only the greatest pastoral elegy in English but also the finest lyric in the language.

The pastoral mode, as found in Spenser and in many of Milton's earlier works, is a key to the poem's unity, which has sometimes been questioned. Older critics often saw the poem as an elegy in which Milton eulogized King and expressed his own personal concerns in digressions on poetry and the church. Most critics today consider these "digressions" central to the poem. The pastoral metaphor allows Milton to apply to King the name "Lycidas" (given by Virgil in his *Eclogues* to a poet-shepherd and by Spenser in *The Shepheardes Calendar* to a Protestant pastor) and represent himself as a shepherd-singer. Clearly the poet's own troubled thought is at the heart of the poem's three-part structure, which moves from a lament for poetic unfulfillment and early death to a lament for bad pastors to an apotheosis of heavenly vision in which love and justice will redress earthly injustice. Lycidas the poet-shepherd becomes Lycidas the priest-shepherd and is transformed into the heavenly guardian of order. Since King, Milton's fellow undergraduate at Cambridge, was to have been a clergyman as well as a poet, it seems both natural and appropriate that poetry (64–84) and pastors (103–31) should be included in the poem. And it is not surprising that Milton, while ostensibly memorializing his Cambridge friend, should think of his own life, with its obvious parallels to King's, as well as of mutability, unfulfilled potential, and the injustice of early death. Joined with the ancient pastoral themes of love, poetry, and death is the Christian viewpoint that affirms the relation between human and divine love, earthly and spiritual consolation. Milton's syncretism makes it possible for supernatural ideas to combine with human concerns, not to replace them, and for Christ the Good Shepherd to represent the reconciling love between man and God. After death—the death of man, nature, poetry—gives way to love and friendship in the elegy, the final consolation leads Milton to a poetic renewal as his persona heads for "pastures new."

Though he was certainly familiar with the reality of death before August 10, 1637, when King drowned in the Irish Sea, this event brought home to Milton the tragic awareness—acutely painful for a developing religious poet—of a young life full of promise cut short. Though not a personal loss, as with Diodati, King's drowning occurred in the same year that his mother died, and writing the poem seems to have been an important working out of emotional issues, a kind of catharsis. After several earlier poems dealing with the deaths of others, "Lycidas" reflects Milton's sense of his own mortality; as he weeps for Lycidas, he weeps for the idea of the poet that Lycidas represents. Most critics see a strong personal element in the poem, though they are not all sure whether the theme of premature death is handled effectively. Samuel Johnson (1709–84) and some modern readers believe that the artificiality of the pastoral prevents the sincere expression of genuine feeling. More to the point is the way in which Milton uses and transforms the pastoral convention.

"Lycidas," clearly more than an elegy for Edward King, transcends the usual elegiac genre, transforming it into a religious and poetic affirmation of life through death. It does so, not by shifting from the pagan to the Christian, as in the "Fair Infant," but by relating these and all the poem's other elements into an integrated whole. Milton's feelings for King, for others, and especially for himself are expressed in imagery of growth and decay, rising and falling, coming and going, and death and resurrection, conveyed in terms of water (of sea and tears), flowers, music, stars, and in the Ovidian myths of Alpheus and Orpheus. Orpheus, traditionally associated with the pastoral elegy, is uniquely seen in "Lycidas" as a rebirth symbol, as a means of affirming good amid tragic loss.

Milton has carefully selected every word and detail to produce what many critics have called the poem's musical precision. He shows himself to be a master not only of sound effects but of a structure of images that echo and reflect each other. " 'Lycidas' has a formal, circular pattern carefully articulated by its rhyme scheme and supportive to its presiding themes."[20] And the tone of the speaker as he circles back and forth over the subject modulates from frustration, despair, and sorrow to exultant relief and consolation based on heavenly hope. Repeated words and ideas ("Lycidas is dead") express emotional intensity and frustration as well as the calmer acceptance of eternal order at the end of the elegy:

> And now the sun had stretched out all the hills,
> And now was dropped into the western bay. (190–91)

Such repetition "emphasizes that poetry is both the means of expressing feeling and of confronting the confusing, even annihilating, forces in the world."[21] The poem offers consolation not simply in its calm ending but in the whole effort to justify the meaning of loss and the tragedy of early death, as the poet moves from doubt to resolution, linking death with the rhythm of nature.

As the beginning of the poem indicates, the death of King is only the occasion for treating universal themes. The speaker is reluctant to write verse before he has reached artistic maturity; but, to eulogize a premature death, he must be willing to risk writing immature poetry. Feeling compelled to fashion from nature a wreath for his deceased friend, to weave the elements of the pastoral elegy into a suitable tribute, he finds the symbols of immortality and poetry, the laurel, ivy, and myrtle, to be unready ("harsh and crude") for the subject. Yet these evergreens, affirming life in the midst of wintry death, also suggest to the reader an implied consolation. The speaker's own unripeness, as well as grief ("Bitter constraint"), is conveyed by intense words (*Shatter, Forc'd*) and suggests his need to take some positive action ("Who would not sing for Lycidas?") to compensate for death. There are strong notes of urgency, harshness, and dissonance in the opening fourteen lines: Nature must be disturbed, for it is indifferent to the reality of suffering. In line 15, the speaker calls upon the Muses, insisting that they not refuse to inspire him in presenting his tribute (the "melodious tear" of line 14); and, if he writes for Lycidas, someone may reward him ("favor my destin'd Urn") with an elegy after his own death.

As the poem makes clear, King, like Milton, was a student and poet who had made a sea journey; Milton too was about to undertake a fifteen-month trip to the Continent. Milton's fears about his own possible death are perhaps part of his revulsion at the whole idea of unfulfillment, represented by King, and of his inner torment as the death of a contemporary brings home to him the injustice in nature. He concludes the first section with a transition to the pastoral theme of Lycidas the shepherd as poet and friend:

> For we were nurst upon the self-same hill,
> Fed the same flock, by fountain, shade, and rill.

If the sadness of life is inevitable, the pastoral offers some comfort in that seasonal death leads to rebirth. But Milton finds the traditional consolations of the pastoral, in which life and death are linked to the rhythm of nature, contradicted by reality. In questioning and violating the idea and convention of the pastoral, Milton denies its comforts before reasserting them in Christian terms at the end. The idyllic harmony of the pastoral only becomes possible in "Lycidas" after the speaker acknowledges negative and discordant feelings. In this poem based on conflict and the disorder caused by death, the tone is agitated, the diction both gentle and harsh as the elegy oscillates between personal and public issues, between innocence and experience, between pagan and Christian elements. According to Rosemond Tuve, "The ebb and flow of love and hostility in the universe is the secret of *Lycidas'* obscure and almost primitive power."[22]

The first section of the elegy itself (25–84) shows that the pastoral "Lawns" of both Cambridge and Arcadia are as indifferent to human suffering and loss as the real world, thus continuing the grim tone of the introduction. The idyllic world of the third verse paragraph celebrates in a generalized way the pleasant expansiveness of the pastoral, but its fresh fields belong to the past, to the memory of an idealized time when the possibility of an old tutor (Damaetas) and his students coming together is gone.[23] As the next paragraph indicates, early death comes to the sheep and flowers before their prime. The "remorseless deep" (50) sharpens the contrast between idyllic and real as the pastoral mode is transformed to express a more realistic view of life. Images of nature that had suggested growth and maturity are replaced by ones suggesting decay and death; this becomes the poem's basic dialectic. The death of Lycidas has destroyed the pastoral as a place of retreat or escape from death, and the nymphs (poets) give no answer to the problem of untimely death.

The poet-speaker's inner conflict, so central to the poem, is captured in the broken lines (56–59) with their frustrated sense of grief and outrage. The lament of "Universal nature" made possible by the Orpheus myth broadens the theme. Since Orpheus symbolized civilization, his death represented a reversion to barbarism, and the poet's own future seems to be equally doomed.

But "Lycidas" invariably offers an opposing strain of thought: Orpheus, whose head and harp floated to the isle of Lesbos, giving the islanders his immortal gift of song, was also a type (foreshadowing) of Christ, whose death brought eternal life.* Thus there is an implication of supernatural consolation, and the pervasive water imagery, with its overtones of the River Jordan, prepares us for the climactic appearance of "him that walked the waves" (173).

But the harsh tone of the next verse paragraph indicates that depression and anger continue to trouble the speaker. What is the use of poetry in the face of death, he asks, especially if I, too, should die before my noble poetic ambition comes to fruition? For the sake of fame, he has chastely avoided erotic, self-indulgent entanglements (Amaryllis and Neaera) and has dutifully prepared himself for a higher calling. He then hears the voice of Phoebus (Apollo), the inspiring sun god, another pagan type of Christ (and parallel to St. Peter later in the poem), who tells the speaker (78–84) that heavenly fame is unrelated to earthly fame: A person is regarded for deeds, not the effect of deeds. This argument with himself through the voice of Phoebus, however, lacks a sense of emotional conviction. Apollo speaks only for pagan poetry, and the elegy embraces a wider vision; and "All-Judging Jove" reflects only an impartial heavenly justice, like that of the Old Testament God, granting to all what they deserve. Dissatisfied, the speaker is ready to attend again to the pastoral world.

In the second section (85–131), an angry attack on corrupt clergy parallels the outburst on poetry and the "thankless Muse" of the first section. In keeping with the organic unity of the poem, water imagery derived from the myth of Alpheus, the river god who pursued Arethusa even after her transformation into a fountain, links the imagery of this section with the earlier references

*The use of the Orpheus myth is important in Milton's poetry. Orpheus, destroyed by the wild, irrational forces of nature, was a symbol of art, reason, and vision in contrast to the natural wildness tamed by his music, which induced universal harmony. But even this great artist, whose mother was a muse, could not escape violent death. Orpheus' murder by drunken worshipers of Bacchus was associated with blind irrationality and chaos. His gentleness and his power to subdue hostile forces made Orpheus a classical analogue of Christ, seen as the true Orpheus, whose descent into Hell paralleled Orpheus' descent to the underworld to rescue Eurydice.

to the sea in which King drowned and in which Orpheus's head floated. Hinting at the ultimate triumph of justice and virtue, symbolized by the reunion of Alpheus and Arethusa, the speaker proceeds with his "Oat" (song), ignoring the glimmer of Christian hope in this pagan myth. He asks if the winds or ocean are to blame for Lycidas's death. The bitterly felt response is that the "fatal and perfidious Bark"—not the water that ultimately cleanses and renews—is responsible. Although nature is not wholly indifferent to man, this answer to the problem of evil seems to offer no more comfort than that provided by the nymphs: The good die young while the bad live on and prosper. Then the image of Lycidas's "sacred" head "sunk so low" in the sea recalls both Orpheus and Alpheus, who hid his head in the sea, and it foreshadows the sun rising from the ocean (167–71), an image that introduces the Son of God, whose power to rise from death to life provides the true consolation. In the cycle of nature, the sun sinks only to return at dawn, affirming continuity both in the nonhuman world of nature, celebrated in the pagan past, and in the human: In the Christian perspective, man is included in the continuity of life that transcends the natural level.

The poet then proceeds from a mythological river to the English river Cam (Cambridge), then to the biblical lake of Galilee, where St. Peter (the "Pilot" of the church, 109) reminds the reader of Christ the Good Shepherd, who cared for his sheep, even selflessly dying for them in order to be reborn. The link between pagan and Christian pastoral is now clear. Peter's "stern" speech with its harsh sounds (122–24), sometimes seen as inappropriate in an elegy, can be considered the climax of the poem since it offers assurance of the Christian consolation to follow. Whereas the sea's cruelty cannot be controlled, cruelty and injustice in religion are human and thus correctable. Peter's outburst "Blind mouths!" recalls the speaker's outburst against "the blind Fury" (fate) at line 75, balancing that earlier personal questioning of vocation with this complaint about abandoning a public vocation. The reader is also expected to make a connection between the destruction of flowers and flocks (45–49) by nature and the "foul contagion" (127) of inner corruption caused by unseeing, uncaring human beings, whose sin reduces them to "blind mouths." Their grating songs and hungry, diseased sheep contrast with the wholesome songs and flocks of authentic shepherd-poets and shepherd-priests. Whereas Nature could only lament at the killing canker, human rapacity and social injustice can be condemned and, ultimately, redressed. The image of the "hungry Sheep" represents a corruption of the idyllic pastoral in the third paragraph. The attack on selfish Anglican clergy who consume rather than feed their flocks, part of the satirical tradition of pastoral poetry, has a harsh tone in keeping with the speaker's mounting rage; he questions the justice that allows parasitical priests to afflict society while good pastors die young. The section concludes with the mysterious image of the "two-handed engine," suggesting that somehow a divine judge holding the scales of justice and mercy will purify the English church. The finality of the comforting words "no more" contrasts with and subtly echoes the poem's opening line.

The third section (132–64) marks an urgent return to the pastoral and the need for a transition from Peter's abusive attack. Alpheus can (and must) return just as flowers can bloom because the voice of judgment has assured the speaker of justice and the church's renewal. Delicate flowers, connoting beauty and love as well as sorrow and death, are listed as tributes to Lycidas; but he is denied a funeral since he lies beneath the "whelming tide." Again, the pastoral rite offers no secure protection against the reality of evil, for the speaker feels that nature does not really weep but is part of the "monstrous world" of evil. For the third time the poem hovers on the brink of nihilism until the turning point when England's guardian angel, St. Michael, is asked to look, not outward, but to Milton's troubled nation:

> Look homeward Angel now, and melt with ruth:
> And, O ye Dolphins, waft the hapless youth.

Nature responds to the speaker's prayer, and though the saint's response is unknown, it is presumably favorable. Rather than shifting suddenly from the pagan level to the Christian, the image of Michael on his mount prepares us for the image of the redeemed Lycidas as the watchful spirit ("Genius," 183) of order that contrasts with the chaos of nature. Lycidas, as the symbol of secure faith as well as art, will now guide all those who wander in the "perilous flood" of doubt, disorder, and corruption. This apotheosis, going beyond traditional Christian consolation, leads to a recognition of grace and mercy in the "blest Kingdoms meek of joy and love" (177). According to Rajan, a form of divine reassurance silences the speaker's outburst of questioning in each part of the poem, culminating in "the higher satisfaction of redemptive love" in Christ, whose power can truly respond to human agony with mercy, not merely justice.[24]

The Christian consolation of the fourth part (the apotheosis of 164–85) comes, then, not as a contrived conclusion but as the only possible answer the poet can find as he boldly questions the cruelty of death and disorder as well as the conventional pastoral means of expressing poetic grief. The masterful blending of emotional experience and pastoral structure produces a resolution in which Lycidas's resurrection and entry into heaven answer the poet's doubts and fears. The speaker's faith enables him to replace his initial treatment of fleeting earthly fame with the eternal, heavenly fame of "other groves, and other streams," recalling Revelation 19.9, where the union of Christ and the sanctified soul is celebrated. The speaker comes to realize that Lycidas was not the pathetic victim of premature death but has been duly taken to his heavenly reward. Chaos is transformed into order: the "wat'ry floor" in which Lycidas sank becomes for Christ and his followers a firm foundation. Milton does not name Christ directly, preferring to relate the waves on which he walked to the once destructive but ultimately comforting waters that are suggested throughout the poem. Merely earthly pastoral has been transformed into Christian pastoral, in which Christ symbolizes harmonizing, universal order; as a result, Lycidas the poet-shepherd and priest-shepherd, free of the vicious acts of wild nature, now hears heavenly music, his soul united with divine love in the "nuptial Song" (176).

In the poem Milton has dramatized his conflicting feelings; his conclusion adds a further dramatic note by revealing that the elegy was spoken by an "uncouth Swain" in a mantle of blue (symbolizing hope and confidence) as he faces a new day with "fresh Woods, and Pastures new." Further poetic achievements lie ahead. The shift to third person distances the poem and its experience, leaving despair behind, for the speaker is now seen to be an observer apart from the persona's emotional turbulence. The poet, who has been at the center of the elegy from the start, has been renewed. The consolation is complete.

# 3

# "My Advent'rous Song": *Paradise Lost*

For his greatest, most ambitious work, Milton chose *the* fundamental story in Western culture, that of Adam and Eve, and the grandest, most demanding genre, the epic. The use of such a familiar story points up the originality of *Paradise Lost,* which dramatically expands the biblical source by imagining characters and episodes beyond human experience. It is conceived on a tremendous scale, with a sense of an immeasurable space beyond our world, and includes a sweeping panorama of past, present, and future. Its many ideas have a universal appeal and indicate the poem's depth, power, and scope. *Paradise Lost* deals with nothing less than the nature of love (divine and human), happiness, marriage, sexuality, laws, dreams, human history, poetry, good, evil, sin, free will, rebellion, death, and immortality, not to mention God and nature itself. It contains features associated with the classical epic—prayers, catalogues, parades of troops, heavenly visitors, visions of the future as well as a pastoral interlude (Books 4–8) and a visit to the underworld (Books 1–2). In scale and style, *Paradise Lost* is perhaps the greatest of epics, but one of its most remarkable features is its difference from other epics. While continually demonstrating his indebtedness to many literary predecessors, Milton asserts that his subject is superior because it is based on the word of God, and is therefore true, and that he has divine inspiration. In *Paradise Lost,* a biblical epic in which he, as well as the reader, plays an important part, Milton forges an entirely new concept of the epic.

## Milton and the Epic

When Milton planned to write a great Christian poem, his first task (as we know from *The Reason of Church Government*) was not to decide what to say but to decide what kind of poem he wanted to create. He carefully considered many possible subjects and genres. In choosing the classical epic form, after abandoning plans for a tragedy, *Adam Unparadised,* he turned to an expression of heroism and grandeur that has long been out of fashion among poets. The epic tradition that Milton inherited begins with Homer but is indebted to Virgil as well as to sixteenth-century Italian poets and to Spenser. The subjects of earlier epics included the legend of King Arthur, the wars of Charlemagne, and, most important, the Trojan War. Thus the epic, a long narrative poem concerning important events, battles, and journeys of adventure, was seen as the noblest form of poetry, surpassing tragedy; it was the means to display a love of magnificence.

Homer's *Iliad* and *Odyssey* (seventh or eighth century B.C.) influenced Virgil, whose *Aeneid* (first century B.C.) became the model for later epics. Virgil looked to the past for inspiration but was influenced by his own society, which had no place for the unbridled individualism of the Homeric adventurer. A greater ideal for Virgil than the individual prowess celebrated by the older, oral (primary) epics was nationalism. For poets of literary (secondary) epics following Virgil, adventure expressed lofty ideals. The simpler world of Achilles or Beowulf, based on fame and valor, was replaced by a new, more complex one.

For Renaissance poets such as Milton, Virgil interpreted the spiritual significance of ancient Rome. His imitators wished to celebrate the glory of their age in the light of enduring spiritual values. Thus Milton, imitating Virgil's broad historical sweep, set out to celebrate human greatness but also to explain what is most important in human life. Since Virgil created an epic in which characters and events represent something beyond themselves, the literary epics descending from him are less concerned with the individual as such than with an ideal person to be emulated—Adam as symbol of mankind, for example, in *Paradise Lost.* The writers of literary epics would agree with Dryden's statement of the purpose of the heroic poem: "to form the mind to heroic virtue by example." The epic had become didactic in a way that Homer's works never were.

Milton's innovations in the epic genre reflect his indebtedness not only to Virgil but to Spenser, whose *The Faerie Queene* (1596) used Arthurian material. Spenser was Milton's principal literary mentor, as he acknowledges in *Areopagitica,* and the first to treat epic material allegorically. Because his personified characters and events stand for moral, religious, or political ideas, he was able to combine classical and Christian elements in a single poem as symbols of truths beyond the literal level of the story. A major influence on Spenser's Christian allegory was the sixteenth-century Italian poem based on the Charlemagne-Roland legend, *Orlando Furioso* by Ariosto, who expanded the epic form to include numerous characters and events. Another Renaissance epic admired by both Spenser and Milton was Torquato Tasso's *Jerusalem Delivered* (1575), an allegorical work about the First Crusade. Tasso's use of Christian angels and devils in place of classical gods helped Spenser develop a Christian poem with supernatural characters. In Milton's lifetime Spenserian imitators such as Giles Fletcher produced Christian epics that treated biblical material in an allegorical as well as classical manner.

Milton builds on these epic traditions but prefers to use a nonallegorical style in juxtaposing Christian and secular ideals to stress the superiority of the Christian ones. He agrees with Tasso that the Christian epic hero should possess the fortitude of Achilles, the wisdom of Aeneas, and the patience of Job but believes that other poets have failed to create heroes who could embody such ethical ideals, for these poets' secular vision of heroism contradicts God's. As John M. Steadman observes, Milton defines heroism negatively by contrasting it with what it is not. It is not, as Satan repeatedly reveals in *Paradise Lost,* physical valor or military adventure. The very fact that Satan is given some traditional heroic attributes reveals Milton's dissatisfaction with the heroic tradition of the epic. Satan's fortitude is seen as rash defiance, his prudence as folly, his leadership as an enslavement.[1] In depicting Satan's journey through Chaos (book 2) as courageous, Milton stresses that mere physical bravery is inadequate and that military valor is destructive. And in his Christian redefinition of epic heroism, Milton challenges the conventional notion of the epic by assigning the leading characteristic of the old heroic ideal—physical valor—to the archfiend. In this way the poet proves that he alone depicts authentic heroism, based on values that the world despises or rejects, especially patience, which Milton defines in *Samson Agonistes* as the "truest fortitude." If Satan represents the false image of wisdom, strength, and prudence, only Christ, often seen as the mystical hero of the epic, can be the true representative of Christian heroism. His love and humility are seen as stronger than the pursuit of any earthly honor.

Many readers of *Paradise Lost* have contended that, although the Son is heroic, the poem lacks a central exemplar of achievement; neither he nor Adam has the qualities of the hero found in the *Aeneid*. Adam and Eve are often seen as the protagonists in the human drama of the poem. As they enact their roles in the moral struggle between the forces of God and Satan, they exemplify man and woman as both sinners and virtuous Christians. Satan is clearly the antihero. The view of Shelley, Blake, and other Romantics that Satan is the hero of the poem is based on the mistaken belief that Milton the rebel must have sympathized with the archrebel. In fact, he created in Satan an antagonist whose stature as a ruined archangel, invested with epic glory, cannot obscure his essential evil. If the hero of *Paradise Lost* is not a particular character but everyone who learns, like Adam and Eve, the lesson of love and suffering, the reader can be said to play that role by fulfilling Milton's claim to improve mankind by improving the individual.[2] The Christian reader addressed in *Paradise Lost* is reminded that true heroism depends on sanctification: Holiness, the result of obedience and suffering after the manner of Christ, makes one heroic. Thus Milton revolutionized the epic tradition by emphasizing human perfectibility and inner regeneration, for the true paradise is not ultimately lost but found within the Christ-like human heart.

## Milton's Style

The style of *Paradise Lost* has been called grand, ornate, sonorous, fluid, remote, musical, muscular, and Latinate, among other things. Critics such as T. S. Eliot have accused Milton of writing English as if it were a dead language and of doing violence to language by "writing poetry at the furthest possible remove from prose."[3] But the epic's elevated language is part of its appeal and suggestiveness; Milton's uncommon subject required an uncommon style—or "styles," for the poem moves and changes as does the poet's handling of language and imagery. The voice of God is markedly different from that of Satan or Adam and Eve; and the narrator's voice, sometimes detached, sometimes immediate and personal, reflects the poet's varied roles as inspired prophet, humble Christian, and moral teacher.

Moreover, Milton follows yet alters the traditional notions of epic decorum, not limiting himself to a single style. As John T. Shawcross notes, the classical epic (based on praise) with its gods, heroes, and great occasions demanded a high style; comedy (based on blame) required a middle style, reflecting its middle-class characters and occasions. The bulk of *Paradise Lost* as it relates to Adam and Eve and their offspring is in this middle style, the high style being reserved for the Father and Son. Satan and his crew, who imagine themselves godlike, are depicted in a falsely high, but really low, style, as befits their pretended heroism.[4] The styles of the poem, then, shift as the characters and subjects develop.

Although Milton's language is consciously literary and removed from everyday prose, it is still related to the spoken word and to the reader's common experience. Such a style, Arnold Stein observes, succeeds in being impersonal and universal while including the individual and personal.[5] It is a style reflecting an indebtedness to Scripture, doctrine, and inspired Christian eloquence as well as an awareness of the poem's grand themes.

Given Milton's purposes, one should not expect dramatic immediacy and metaphor in the Shakespearean sense. The dignity of both the epic genre and the subject are not compatible with startlingly fresh metaphors. Milton's verse is rooted in ancient materials and in a view of poetry as public statement. In *Of Education,* he speaks of poetry as having three characteristics: it should be simple (having intellectual clarity), sensuous (reflecting sense perceptions), and passionate (having sustained energy).

The appropriateness in *Paradise Lost* of a heightened style with its seemingly artificial language and syntax has often been noted. "*Paradise Lost* improves on other epics by dealing not simply with events that surpass the ordinary, but with events that transcend and initiate the world we know. The distance is therefore the maximum possible and the style must be heightened accordingly."[6] And Joseph Summers reminds us that Milton's readers cannot be allowed to forget "that the poem does not directly concern human beings like themselves and that its action is the greatest possible one."[7] Thus readers must not be distracted by familiar scenes or colloquial voices. The poem must appeal to our experience and responses yet transcend them.

To consider such an epic style too grand or lacking in intimacy, C. S. Lewis observes, is to accuse it of being what it is supposed to be. He observes that a "ritual" style is important in such a secondary epic because individual readers will not feel any of the solemnity experienced by the hearers of a primary epic unless they feel they are participating in an august ritual. "The Virgilian and Miltonic style is there to compensate for—to counteract—the privacy and informality of silent reading."[8] The elevated style is achieved mainly by three means: the use of many unfamiliar words and constructions; the use of proper names, suggesting splendid, remote, or celebrated things; and sensory allusions and images. The diction is familiar yet special; the style is thus an aspect of the ceremonial dignity expected of an epic. Such a style may blind us, C. M. Bowra says, to the great emotional effects of the poem. The classicism of form and the grandeur of language can prevent us from seeing that the work is deeply felt and has a powerful life that more superficially attractive poetry lacks.[9]

Milton may seem to state rather than suggest, but, when we finish reading or hearing a passage, we often see that he suggests more than we at first suspect. His is a densely allusive style. His syntax, an influence on many later poets, allows direct meaning to coexist with implication. For example, Adam in Book 5 whispers to the sleeping Eve, "her hand soft touching": Is her hand soft or does he touch it softly? That both meanings are simultaneously possible indicates a rich ambiguity that allows the poet to imply more than he states. Sometimes a line causes us to stop and read both ways: "The Fiend / Walk'd up and down alone bent on his prey" (3.441) indicates that Satan is both alone in his walking and single-minded in his plot. A separation in the usual word order ("tore / Through pain up by the roots" 2.543–44) can heighten the sense of violence, as in the picture of Satan's fall at 1.44–47, where the separation of *Him* and *down* suggests physical movement.

Great pictures and themes are conveyed by long, flowing sentences in which dramatic tension is heightened by puns that add ingenuity to his metaphors ("puny infantry") and presuppose our knowledge of Latin etymologies. As a result, he can use words with special force to define and emphasize ideas. As Christopher Ricks observes, Milton's use of Latinate words does not mean that the English meaning is discarded in favor of grandiose substitutions; what seems like pedantry is in fact an additional resonance whereby some words (*transported, commotion*) can express a sense of physical movement.[10]

Milton has been accused of emphasizing sound at the expense of image or idea, yet his visual sense and indebtedness to painting and architecture have been conclusively demonstrated. His style is often called baroque because of its sense of energetic movement, spatial illusion, ornate structure, and dramatic conflicts. His sound effects, moreover, are part of an organic style in which thought and expression are one; they are not superimposed on previously established images but are responsible for the great pictures every reader sees in the poem. The poet tends to see things in motion, with a painter's sense of depth and breadth rather than with a camera's focus.[11] See, for example, the description of paradise at 4.246–68 or of the fallen angels marching across Hell's burning soil at 1.544–47, where the tense shift creates an illusion, like that of foreground in painting, of the banners rising against a background of darkness.

A striking feature of Milton's style in *Paradise Lost* is the innovative use of epic similes, which are "more frequent, longer, more complex and more meaningful than those of any other epic poet."[12] These elaborate images, sometimes forming miniature scenes, introduce materials from Milton's reading and experience that call attention to the poet and his presence in the poem; they take us briefly out of the poem, sometimes helping us visualize the unimaginable. As Broadbent points out, the epic simile, like a landscape background in a painting, has a window-opening effect and often involves us in relating a familiar image from our experience to the poem's unfamiliar world. For Milton's contemporary readers, the geographical and other materials used in similes were of value and interest. From Milton's vast reading came information on giants, monsters, comets, stars, ships, and birds—all of which appear in descriptions of Satan. Satan seems so important in the poem in part because "he has more epic similes and other imagery attached to him than any other subject in the poem."[13]

Other stylistic devices include ellipsis ("Who can think [of] submission?"), periphrasis ("moving fires" for stars), repetition, catalogues or lists, epithets, double negatives, and longer sentences.

Milton's blank verse is not simply unrhymed iambic pentameter but involves many heavily stressed lines in which rhythm is determined by sense: "Forthwith upright he rears from off the pool" (1.221). The effect can suggest violent action or physical motion or a sense of nature's lush, richly endowed beauty (as at 4.258–62). Such passages reveal Milton's poetry as simple, sensuous, and passionate.

## Ideas in Milton

Milton's poetry is inseparable from his ideas, which include some complex issues of belief. In contrast to the Calvinists, Milton did not display any contempt for the flesh, distrust of human reason, contempt for natural law, or belief in human depravity. He was an individualist in an age of sharply defined religious factions. The poet's theological positions are not always consistent in his work as a whole or even within *Paradise Lost*. Although Milton has God the Father pronounce an apparently Calvinist view of predestination, for example, his own position is closer to that of the theologian Arminius (1560–1609), who emphasizes free will over predestination. In general, Milton tends to be more optimistic about the nature of man than his Protestant contemporaries, and his sometimes unorthodox Christianity owes more to traditional, medieval theology, especially that of St. Augustine, than to much seventeenth-century doctrine. A basic Miltonic tenet is that theological orthodoxy is incompatible with the freedom the Christian needs to cultivate virtue.

As a Christian epic, *Paradise Lost* assumes the reader's familiarity with many doctrines, some of which are briefly outlined here, and with certain religious paradoxes, such as freedom through obedience, glory through shame, life through death, happiness through suffering, strength in weakness, and the fortunate fall (the redemption, enabling fallen man to be saved). Other ideas are treated more specifically in the detailed commentary that follows.

1. God created all things good, evil being the absence of good. He created the universe from Himself, not out of nothingness. Thus the universe is an infinitely expanding circle of goodness outside of which no created being can exist.
2. Goodness includes free will, from which evil arises. Evil things are good things perverted by a conscious creature who chooses the self rather than God. Satan, the first creature more interested in himself than in obeying God, was guilty of the sin of pride. Milton depicts sin in different ways in the epic. In heaven, Sin is metaphorically generated from Satan's mind in an internal, free act of self-determination with no prior cause. After man's fall, evil becomes an inheritance affecting all people. Between these polarities are Adam and Eve, who choose evil yet are externally affected (tempted) by it.
3. Original sin resulted from man's original freedom by which Eve allowed herself to be tempted by the serpent and Adam allowed himself to be tempted by Eve. Since Eve was weaker, being created from Adam, she gave in to the tempter's seduction, whereas Adam's sin was greater because he sinned against reason in choosing to follow Eve rather than God. For Milton, Adam and Eve were real, historical beings. As a result of their Fall, all of creation was corrupted and evil came into the world.
4. Milton follows the traditional church teaching of St. Augustine that good can exist without evil (as in Heaven) but that evil cannot exist without good and that good and bad angels have the same nature, which is "happy when it adheres to God and miserable when it adheres to itself."[14] Hence the distinction between the brilliance of Satan's nature in the poem as opposed to his perverted will. As Lewis points out, "If no good (that is, no being) at all remained to be perverted, Satan would cease to exist."[15]
5. Although God is good and makes creatures who reflect his goodness, He foreknows that some angels and men will voluntarily choose evil and that He will turn their evil to good.

This foreknowledge, existing outside of human time, does not determine the free action of these creatures. Rejecting Calvinist predestination, Milton puts great emphasis on free will and reason.

6. The Christian needs right reason, which is different from ordinary human reason. Right reason is the discriminating moral faculty implanted in all men as a guide to truth. Douglas Bush calls it a rational and philosophical conscience that distinguishes man from the beasts and links man with man and with God, enabling him to have some understanding of God, who is perfect reason.[16]
7. Although Milton's Fall is seen as a complex of sins, he follows the traditional teaching of Augustine and other church fathers in believing that the initial sin consisted of disobedience but resulted from pride. Because of man's disobedience he became subject to powerful passions that threaten the legitimate preeminence of reason.
8. Obedience and love are inseparable on Earth and in Heaven. To obey God's law and not to eat of the Tree of Knowledge is to obey the unwritten law of temperance, which keeps man in his middle place between angels and beasts on the chain of being. Disobedience prevents man from understanding God, which is for Milton the ultimate aim of all inquiry. Obedience is the key to freedom, which begins with God as long as fallen man chooses to follow Scripture.
9. Had there been no Fall, man would have been raised to angelic status in Heaven since created goods are constantly being perfected in a movement upward toward God.
10. In not clearly distinguishing between matter and spirit, Milton deviated from standard Christian teaching. According to his philosophy of monism, spirit is a refinement of matter, and matter, a debased form of spirit, is ever becoming spiritual.
11. Among Milton's unorthodox beliefs is his view of the Christian Trinity: The Son is not seen as having equal status with the Father. He did not exist from all eternity and is not omniscient. The Son and Holy Spirit are depicted in the poem largely as divine agents of the Father's love and wisdom, respectively. In describing God in human terms, Milton reflects the belief that, although man cannot know

God as He truly is, the Bible is the best guide to the way He wishes to be understood.

12. Heaven is a realm of light in which God and angels dwell in perfect bliss. Angels, whom Milton believed to be immortal spirits created long before our universe, are given various tasks as messengers, guardians, and warriors, but are otherwise not extensively described. Milton's Hell is more complex, a specific place yet one remote from our world. Milton usually thought of Hell as psychological, an inner state of being. But he believed that Heaven and Hell will outlast the physical universe, and, without denying their existence as historically real places, he can imagine them as spiritual states.

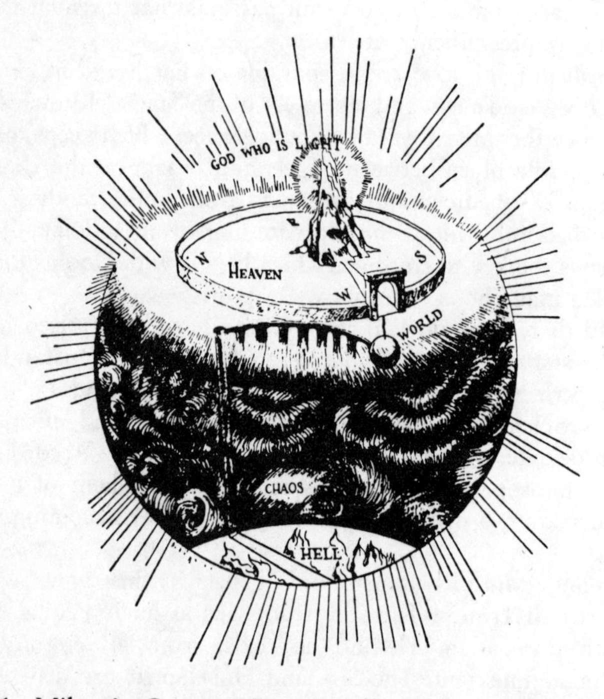


Fig. 1. Milton's Cosmos. Drawing by Walter Clyde Curry in Merritt Y. Hughes, editor, *John Milton: Complete Poems and Major Prose* (New York: Odyssey, 1957).

## *Paradise Lost*

## *Commentary*

### Book 1

The opening prayer for inspiration declares at once the subject of the poem: "Man's first disobedience," the sin of Adam and Eve, the first in a long line of human transgressions of God's will. This invocation concludes with Milton's stated purpose: to assert Providence, as opposed to fate, and "to justify [reveal the justice of] the ways of God to men." That is, the poet will explain nothing less than the cause of evil in the world and how it can coexist with an all-good creator. He will do so by tracing the causes of Adam and Eve's expulsion from the Garden of Eden and by showing how their fall was fortunate in allowing Christ the Redeemer to come. Without the Redemption, sin would make no sense in a world governed by a merciful God; with the Redemption, Christ, the unique "Man" (4), will restore us to "our Seat" or heavenly home. Milton believes that the earlier, parallel fall of Satan and the other rebel angels was also fortunate since it provided the basis for the fall of man, resulting in the self-sacrifice of the Son as redeemer.

That the poet is aware of his unique and ambitious undertaking is clear: he states that his poem will soar in high style ("no middle flight") since it deals with what no poet has yet attempted. This is not a boast but a fact. As a Christian epic, *Paradise Lost* will boldly surpass the valorous exploits celebrated by pagan poets and redefine the nature of epic heroism. Its scope will include both the whole universe and the mind of the individual—the poet and the reader. It will raise such issues as life and death, good and evil, love and hate, as well as sin, salvation, free will, temptation, happiness, sexuality, and the origins of society and history. The characters are also unique: the poem will not, for the most part, describe people as the reader knows them from either experience or literature.

That the poet needs heavenly enlightenment for such an undertaking is more than mere convention. His muse (later called Urania, the conventional patroness of astronomy) stands for the divine inspiration that revealed God's truths to Moses at Oreb and Sinai and represents the spirit of God in each believer. God's inspirational force is associated with Sion, the sacred temple of Jerusalem and symbol of the Chosen People, and with Siloa's brook (John 9.1–12), where the blind man was miraculously made to see, a revealing parallel to the narrator's plea for insight. The poet's task is seen as greater than anything the classical muses of "th' *Aonian* mount" (Mount Helicon) were ever called upon to aid, for, as Summers says, the narrator knows what readers know, yet he must also be prophetic and inspired, telling them what no narrator could know or have witnessed: the Fall. The invocation, with its shifts in tense indicating the poem's timeless reference, sets this familiar story in a context that includes all time yet begins before time and ends after it, with the Last Judgment.[17]

Milton then calls upon the Spirit of God specifically, for since the poet wishes to explain Christian revelation, he must be nourished with insight into God's mysteries. So this invocation is a prayer more than simply a call for poetic aid. The brooding, breeding spirit impregnating the deep at the creation of the world (Genesis 1.2) is called upon to illuminate the poet's darkened vision and so lift or exalt his low level of earthly understanding so he can rise to the height of insight demanded by his great subject ("Argument"). The poem's central polarities of light-dark and ascent-descent are thus sketched in this invocation.

From the outset, the poem presents a careful pattern of woe and joy, loss and restoration. It begins, not with a celebration of heroic deeds but with "disobedience," "death," "woe," and "loss"; but soon shifts to the more hopeful "restore" and "regain" because of Christ, the "one greater Man" whose sacrificial death on the cross will redeem the sin of Adam and his descendants. The epic is based on the central Christian doctrine of the Incarnation: the Son of God becomes man to provide salvation for all generations of believers, a greater good thus coming out of the initial evil. Some of these ideas are indicated by Milton's initial wordplay: *fruit* not only recalls the forbidden fruit of the Tree of Knowledge (Genesis 2.17) but also means *result; mortal* means both *deadly* and "making men mortal" since the sin of Adam and Eve is seen as the cause of human weakness: primeval man lost the perfection of Eden, suffering disease and death as the result of his first disobedient act. Obedience will be a central lesson for Adam and Eve and for Milton's intended reader, whose education in Christian virtues is basic to the poem's purpose.

Since Milton will show how Adam and Eve turned away from God, beginning the poem with Satan is a necessity if the reader is to understand the effects of the fallen angels' sinful rebellion. Satan's entrance into the poem is startling: he has just fallen (44) as though shoved through a trapdoor in Heaven. His downfall has resulted in a humanly understandable torment. Milton touches on the cause of this torment only briefly (Satan's "obdurate pride and steadfast hate") but then describes the indescribable "darkness visible" of Hell because it is not the poet's intention to present the evil aspects of Satan at this point, only his suffering and determination to persist in opposing God.

Although Milton calls Satan "infernal Serpent" at line 34, the fallen angel first appears with much of his celestial brilliance, and the reader is not immune to his appeals. From the start, a true view of the father of lies and enemy of mankind is easily obscured by a sense of admiration for his seemingly heroic greatness. Milton, familiar with defeat, rebellion, and frustrated anger, invests his rebel angels with some of his own feelings. But the context of Hell and Satan's rhetoric prevent any real sympathy with Satan, who has been romanticized by some readers as a defiant, Promethean hero, majestic in defeat. His first speech, with its broken syntax (line 84) conveying his emotional confusion and disorientation, initially suggests a humanized, sympathetic character; but his illogical rhetoric reveals his self-delusion behind the glorious facade. He falsely claims to have shaken God's throne, but the war was waged with Michael, not God. Clearly, Satan's pride is undiminished, though he recognizes the loss of his apparent "luster." Since he claims that only a "field" (battle) has been lost, he pretends that the war is not over: "All is not lost," though he has just lamented his misery and ruin. He believes that his courage and invincible will make him God's evenly matched adversary whose "substance cannot fail": thus he is too proud to stoop or kneel to the Almighty. Even while his angelic substance is deteriorating as he speaks, he does not want to recognize that God controls his fate and that he cannot hope to win in any battle with God. He claims to be indomitable when, in fact, he is clearly overcome. Satan's proud assertion that God is a tyrant reveals his impotence. He makes it seem as if God had been an underdog in the heavenly war who won by a fluke, as if Satan can choose to make the best of what he lost. The reader, made aware of the irony, is told of Satan's false front: he has been "vaunting" (boasting) amid his deep despair.

When Beelzebub, the second most powerful of the fallen angels, asks how they should respond to God's obviously omnipotent force, Satan responds that they must do only evil. He thinks, with the battle having just ended, that the worst is now over and that in a council the fallen angels should discuss ways that would "most offend / our enemy." But they cannot "repair" the loss or regain "Hope," as redeemed man is allowed to do. *Loss* and *lost* are echoed in Satan's speeches as he tries to grasp the immense horror of what he has thrown away. Yet, as Louis L. Martz observes, Satan does not seem entirely wicked or lost until he loses the sense of hope, until it is seen that he has no future except meaningless destruction. One obvious sign of ultimate hope for man—a sign that Satan has *not* succeeded in destroying mankind—is the sense of admiration for Satan's fallen brilliance; then the reader is shown the larger context of Hell from which Satan cannot escape, having sealed his own fate by choosing to continue to do evil, and realizes that Books 1 and 2 reveal a vain and futile insurrection. As Satan expresses hate, the narrator expresses love and hope in a counterpoint that is one of the epic's major innovations: Milton, with his dual emphasis on hope and despair, destruction and regeneration, keeps alive a sense of hope even amid the loss.[18]

Yet hopelessness is an essential element in the depiction of Hell, where disorder and disintegration are predominant; it is a world of paradox where fire and flood are compatible ("fiery deluge") and where darkness is "visible." It is described negatively, as a place where peace never comes. The perception of Hell is a disorienting experience not only for Satan but for the reader, who sees the underworld through Satan's eyes. As Hughes notes, "Milton usually thought of Hell as psychological and nonlocal. . . . At its most intense he imagined it in the heart of Satan." But he believed that Heaven and Hell will outlast the physical universe and that they could be imagined as spiritual states so long as their existence as historical places is not denied.[19] As is seen in Books 1 and 2, the Hell of *Paradise Lost,* less understandable than Dante's in the *Inferno,* is an unfamiliar, ambiguous realm beyond normal human experience.

As we are introduced to the varied landscape of Hell and to the other fallen angels, we see that Milton's purpose is to make evil concrete and the devils' new abode imaginatively "real" and comprehensible. Milton separates yet continually relates human and heavenly history, asking the reader to consider the parallel between the newly fallen angels and man, who is still unfallen in his recently created world.

Satan, a master of accommodation, creates and occupies an imaginary mental world in which God "now triumphs" as Satan's unjust adversary. His sense of independent freedom is a futile self-sufficiency that mocks true independence. Beelzebub shares his chief's delusion, believing that the rebel angels "endangered" and tested God's supremacy, a logical impossibility. How could the "perpetual King" be endangered? By asserting God's supremacy, Beelzebub undercuts his speech with contradictory arguments; the fallen angels see themselves as gods, or independent beings, making their efforts to defy God comically absurd. Beelzebub recognizes the reality of defeat but retains pride in the apparent angelic freedom from annihilation. When he begins to realize (153–55) that eternal punishment is a dubious award, Satan quickly responds with a specious claim to choose evil; perverting God's goodness is the only possible "delight" simply because it negates God's will. The rebel angels have lost the freedom to do good and the freedom to choose because of their earlier choice in Heaven not to obey God. Though there is no possibility of hope, his speech ends with a typically specious proposal to discuss how this disaster might be repaired. There is a sad irony in Beelzebub's attitude, for he who stood in God's presence as one of the highest-ranking angels never understood something fundamental about God: that he does not keep or make slaves.

As Lewis observes, Satan is a magnificent character, not because he is a great creature but because he is a creature portrayed in a grand manner.[20] He is made to appear both mighty and splendid. Lying on the fiery lake, Satan is described in the first of the great epic similes of *Paradise Lost* as huge, as "long and large" as classical monsters, including Typhon or the biblical sea monster, Leviathan. His heroic size represents his former angelic greatness, yet Satan is also described as a "bulk" floating like cargo in the water, an image that deflates his grandeur. Milton, extending the simile to include a more familiar scene, pictures a mariner mistaking the leviathan-whale for an island, so the simile becomes a digression on the false security of trusting wholly in earthly things. Such a rich combination of classical, biblical, and folklore does more than convey Satan's gigantic size: it brings the readers into the poem and into the poet's world, and it forces them to decide how to visualize what is unvisualizable. The speaker's voice explains that God's permissive will allows Satan to pursue "his own dark designs" but that from this evil will come "Infinite goodness" for man. The poet's voice, reminding the reader of the more hopeful aspect of the Christian story, is always an important counterpoint to the rendering of evil.

In the next picture, Satan, like the mariner foolishly tied to the great whale, is himself "Chain'd" on the burning lake. Flying from liquid fire to solid fire, he imagines that, as a god (angel), he has escaped the worst part of Hell by his own strength rather than, as the epic voice says, by God's design. God knows that all of Satan's actions can bring about at most only an interruption of divinely established order. Surveying the "mournful gloom," he accepts it, trying to establish his own sovereignty, security, and freedom. That he does so in such a grisly setting, with such pretended grandeur, is absurd. He claims that God, a tyrant, is his equal and that he has the freedom to choose (261) the horrors that he is condemned to suffer, never admitting that God controls his actions.

Speaking to Beelzebub as the self-proclaimed leader, Satan says that in Hell "We shall be free" and then, with a flourish of unreality, declares, "Better to reign in Hell, than serve in Heav'n." He suggests that their "faithful friends" not be left lying in oblivion but called to "share" in the dubious discovery of their misery and of what more may be lost. One wonders why they should revive at the sound of their leader's voice when that leader so disastrously misled them.

In likening Satan's shield hanging on his shoulders to the moon, Milton includes specific contemporary references that alter the reader's perception of the fallen archangel: suddenly the moon's sphere is seen magnified through the telescope of Galileo. His spear, far larger than a Norwegian pine, has become a cane or crutch with which he supports himself as he walks over the burning ground. And Satan's legions lie enchanted, as thick as piles of autumn leaves not only in the shady valley (Vallombrosa) that Milton visited in Italy but also in the work of earlier poets (Homer, Virgil, Dante). The images of leaves and water allude to classical and biblical sources, specifically the masses of seaweed in the Red Sea where Pharaoh and his men were overcome as they, too, tried to thwart God's purposes (Exodus 14). The picture is one of numberless angels reduced to base destruction and loss in contrast to what is in store for God's favored people. Despite the "hideous change" from their former glory, the fallen angels are addressed sarcastically with their old titles as the "Flow'r of Heav'n," for Satan is trying to rouse them with his resounding voice. He does so by goading them to "Awake, rise, or be forever fall'n" (330), when, in fact, they are eternally lost, and suggests that God may catch them lying in Hell and destroy them utterly. They spring up like sleepy men, blindly obeying their "general's voice"; their sinning against heavenly obedience has reduced them to the forced obedience of slavery. The image of Moses calling up the cloud of locusts to darken Egypt (Exodus 10) suggests both the size and number of "those bad Angels" and their enslavement to the "Sultan," a name connoting the dark forces of pagan tyranny. The legions are also compared to hordes of Germanic tribes that overwhelmed Roman civilization, a foreshadowing of future evils in human history.

Before the Homeric catalogue or listing of the devils (381–505), Milton recalls the vestiges of their grandeur, reminding the reader that the Fall of Man could only have been perpetrated by superior powers. Merritt Y. Hughes says:

> The catalogue of devils rests on a widely accepted belief, coming down from antiquity, that in ancient times the devils deceived mankind and usurped God's worship by masquerading as the gods of the pagan world. . . . In Milton's roll-call of devils their later careers as pagan deities let them appear under the names of the gods whom the prophets denounced for seducing Israel.[21]

Milton's readers would have recognized these names, which denote evil spreading throughout the world, and would have seen the parallel between God's chosen people in the Old Testament and themselves as the Christians of the New. Of special importance in this list are two spirits who participate in the Council

(Book 2): Moloch, cruel sun god of the Ammonites (2 Kings 23), and the god of lust, Belial. Michael's prophetic view of history in Books 11 and 12 of *Paradise Lost* clarifies the importance of this list.

Relieved to see that they have not been annihilated, the fallen angels find some joy in their leader's hopeful countenance, but the reader knows that they are misled, for Milton has cited Satan's despair. Raising their "fainting courage" with hollow rhetoric, Satan orders martial music as his standard (the symbolic antithesis of Christ's victorious cross) is proudly raised in a rich description of the military valor associated with ancient heroes (551–53) with whom the devils are ironically likened. Suddenly in the darkness gleam ten thousand banners and a forest of spears as the devils march to the bestial music of woodwinds. In "guise / Of Warriors old" they stand, the demonic counterpart of the host of Heaven. A formidable force, they would make a human army resemble pygmies (575), even if the armies of ancient and medieval legend were included. If the assembled force surpasses even the most heroic human capability, the towering Satan is even more awesome than any man, his angelic brightness dimmed yet still shining, his face scarred by "Thunder." Care and sorrow have riven him, and his heart burns within him as he realizes the immense loss into which he has led his followers; they were, and remain, faithful to him, although they were blasted, like tall forests on a mountainside struck by lightning. As he surveys the host before him, their glory "Wither'd," proud, vengeful Satan has a moment of remorse ("Millions of Spirits for his fault amerc't [deprived] / Of Heav'n") as he struggles to speak.

In a grand oration he reassures those whom he misled that the struggle was noble even if the outcome ("event") was disastrous. Flattering his audience and diverting its attention from his responsibility for their misery, he finds it incredible that such matchless forces, which he falsely claims "emptied Heav'n," could be repulsed and could fail to repossess their home (633–34). These lines point up an important thematic contrast in the poem between the pride of ascent and the humility of descent. Messiah will be exalted by the Father in order to be humiliated as the suffering servant before being restored to the Father's right hand. His pattern of obedient love, the antithesis of Satan's rebellious hate, is seen in the poem as the central lesson for Adam, who also aspires to be Godlike and in sinning falls. But man's fortunate fall leads to the promise of a reascent to God not possible for the fallen angels.

Satan, now directing his followers' anger to God, pictures Him as a figurehead whose power was attributable to mere tradition, until challenged by the rebels, and whose real strength was concealed; thus he says it was God who led the angels into revolt and caused their fall (642). Satan uses empty arguments to depict God's authority as empty. Aware of God's power, which he has just questioned, Satan abandons his goal of retaking Heaven and proposes a plan that better suits his present resources: to investigate the heavenly rumor about a new race supposedly equal to the angels. Convinced that nothing can restrain the fallen spirits, Satan does not know if he can venture outside Hell. Thus he says that, rather than fear more war, the devils should secretly work to subvert God's new creation: peace is seen as impossible since submission is unthinkable. Applauding Satan's battle cry the fallen angels hurl futile defiance against Heaven.

Under the lead of Mammon, the least upright ("erect") of all the fallen angels, a group of demons sets out to dig for mineral riches. Milton's epic voice intrudes to remind the reader not to be surprised that such "riches grow in Hell." The introduction of Mammon, who personifies materialism, leads to Milton's warning that, no matter how great human achievements may be, they are impermanent when contrasted with immortal, particularly diabolic, powers.

The building of the great temple of Pandemonium (Milton's word for "home of all the demons"), the "high Capitol" of Hell, looks forward to Adam's later vision (in Book 11) of self-directed human achievements and so is linked with the theme that evils in human history arise from misusing God's gifts. Throughout the poem, evil results from a self-centered, rather than God-centered attitude. The spirits admire the grandeur of the vast building, failing to see its idolatrous excess, its gaudy mixture of architectural styles. Its architect, Mammon, is equated with Mulciber (Vulcan or Hephaestus), Milton using classical myth for his own purposes: Mulciber's legendary fall from Heaven recalls Satan's expulsion from Heaven and anticipates the loss of Paradise by Adam and Eve.

As heralds proclaim the upcoming Council and as the spirits flock into the crowded Capitol, the reader sees that Hell is a limited, enclosed place, Pandemonium being its innermost part. As they swarm into the "spacious Hall," the fallen angels are compared to bees, their significance trivialized by imagery that recalls the *Iliad.* (2.87–90) and the *Aeneid* (1.430–36). The bee simile conveys not only the number of the devils and their hissing noise but also their futile "busyness." It also suggests that Pandemonium is only a "Straw-built Citadel" where the beelike demons are attracted to vanity as bees to pollen, and they gossip like absurd, amateur politicians. The simile prepares for the devils' diminution in size as they use their power to change shape; their minute stature is now compared to that of pygmies or elves as seen (or imagined) by a peasant, the simple human image again making the scene more accessible while also implying that evil diminishes the spirits. Meanwhile, in the inner chamber Satan and his lieutenants, monumental as ever, are eager to continue plotting.

## Book 2

The Council in Pandemonium opens with Satan enthroned amid Eastern opulence and pagan luxury, reflecting his intemperance and exhibitionism. The trappings of royalty, abhorrent to Milton the antimonarchist, are exaggerated so that, in an ironic reversal of the ascent-descent pattern, Satan is "exalted" by bad "merit" to the height of evil; he aspires beyond despair to pursue "Vain War with Heav'n," having learned nothing from his recent insurrection. Milton depicts a world where everything is upside down so that what is especially high is, from God's perspective, abysmally low.

The inconsistencies in Satan's speeches show that his character develops and changes as he assumes various roles. He is sometimes the independent instigator of his own actions; when God withdraws and allows him to act, we sense that he is more than a puppet. Yet Milton's interventions qualify our perception of him as a free dramatic character. Milton allows the demons to glorify themselves while simultaneously unmasking the pretentious nature of their self-evaluation. In his initial speech in the so-called debate, Satan claims that Heaven is not lost, yet he earlier accepted Hell and said farewell to Heaven (1.242–63). The fallen archangel pretends that his descent was voluntary and prepares for a reascent since he thinks that, because of their fall, the devils will be more "glorious" than unfallen angels and so will not fall again. The reader knows that man, unlike the angels, was both led astray and redeemed by external means, not by his own power. For the fallen angels, there is no repentance, grace, or restoration, and Satan's aim will be to reverse the *felix culpa* (happy sin) and bring evil out of good.

Satan, the self-appointed leader, then asserts his varying claims to sovereignty: that the laws of Heaven (which he has scorned) ordained him leader; that the free choice of those who followed his rebellion makes him superior; and that, lest his audience question these dubious claims, his natural preeminence or "merit" makes him deserve the first place, though a few lines later (32–33), he will assert that no one will claim precedence in Hell since its pain makes precedence unenviable. He who claimed that it was better to reign in Hell than serve in Heaven (1.263) also says that occupying the highest place "exposes" him to the greatest danger from God's retribution. Seeing that it is useless to engage in competitive strife now that Heaven has been lost, he clearly wants to remain in charge. Taking a selective look at the fallen angels' predicament, he will not openly admit to its desperation since that might lead to calls for his dethronement. The irrationality of the satanic mind is here fully revealed: the "advantage" of the pain that torments Satan and his followers is that it unites them in a common purpose, one based on the fear of further punishment.

First to follow Satan in the infernal Council is the ruthless Moloch, the "furious King" of the battle in Heaven (6.357) who is so consumed by ambition that he would rather be dead than conquered. Caring only for his own fierce reputation, Moloch reflects Satan's own desperate "Monarchal pride" (428), calling for "open War" so that Hell's tortures can be used against "our Torturer." The theme of his speech reflects the rebel angels' vainglorious urge for supremacy and the irrational nature of evil central to the poem. Though they have no other alternative, the demons go through the motions of deciding, as Moloch does, that dwelling in Hell is worse than fighting, which, he says, cannot worsen their plight. He tries to answer objections to his view by noting that angels naturally ascend (descent is difficult); this argument, ironically, is based on the very hierarchy against which he rebels. Because of their experience ("proof") of defeat, Moloch says in a final burst of illogic, his cohorts should feel themselves strong enough to "disturb" God's "fatal" (unshakable) throne, thereby unwillingly admitting the ineffectuality of the action he has advocated.

Belial is more gracious in bearing ("act") than Moloch, but Milton says that the fair appearance of this demon is deceptive. Belial refutes Moloch's militaristic arguments, stating that they are based on despair and that revenge against God is futile. Expressing with pathos the sense of loss these spirits feel, Belial asks why they should bother to challenge God's impregnable power only to lose their being, their ability (painful though it is) to think and feel. Why, he asks, risk worsening our condition since sitting and consulting are better than fighting or facing even worse horrors in an eternity of woe? Since God cannot be defeated or deceived, Belial reasons, war is unrealistic: the fallen angels really have no alternative but to accept what strength they have. This view of God undercuts his next point: that they patiently endure in the hope that the "supreme Foe" may lessen his ire and show some mercy. Thus advocating "peaceful sloth," Belial uses various rhetorical tricks, including illusory promises, ridicule, and sarcasm to respond to the warmongering spirits for whom Moloch is the spokesman.

Mammon then advocates peace also for selfish reasons, first dismissing the possibility of unseating God and regaining Heaven. He proudly scorns the idea that God might "relent," for this would entail "new Subjection." Ironically standing before Satan enthroned, he rejects the idea of the slavery of Heaven, where the fallen spirits would be forced to sing the praises of the enthroned "Sovran" in endless submission. Since force is impossible, they must seek their "own good" for themselves, as if they are free "and to none accountable." Mammon seems to think, like Belial, that with some effort evil can be made bearable. He extends Belial's wishful thinking about accommodation with a recommendation for building a rival empire of "order" and "peaceful safety" where they can (impossibly) thrive, ignoring Heaven.

The councillors prefer Mammon's suggestion because they dread a return to combat and are captivated by the thought of becoming empire builders. Their satisfaction lasts only as long as it takes for Beelzebub to stand and refute Mammon's argument. Beelzebub ("lord of the flies"), next to Satan "in power and next in crime" (1.79), seems princely as he is about to advocate his "devilish Counsel," but Milton emphasizes his ruined majesty. As lines 379–85 and 466–73 indicate, Satan and Beelzebub have rigged the debate. Beelzebub counters the favorably received speeches of Belial and Mammon by challenging the "princes of Hell" not to imagine they can escape their misery for more comfortable dreams; he presents a picture of enslavement and punishment yet also speaks of revenge. Since the fallen spirits cannot alter God's eternal power, they can more subtly undermine His creation, "an easier enterprise" than invading impregnable Heaven. In Book 1 (162–65), Satan has hinted at the plot to fight God by seducing man, something only the "Author of all ill" could devise. According to a heavenly rumor ("fame"), another world is to be created for man, who is falsely seen by Beelzebub as more favored than the angels, thus implying that God is foolish to favor a lesser being.

The Satan-Beelzebub plan is either to ruin man's world or to have the future race of God's "darling sons" join the devils in opposing the Almighty, who would destroy man, thus ruining God's "joy" in punishing the evil spirits. The conclusion of Beelzebub's speech couples Hell and Earth, where sin will wreak havoc but not destruction.

With his proposal easily adopted, Beelzebub proceeds, offering a vain hope of being uplifted and dreaming the vain dreams he had earlier scorned: of reentering, or at least approaching, Heaven. His contrived question of "whom to send" on the arduous trip to the new world stresses the physical perils associated with epic heroes' great journeys; the venture will require strength and subtlety.

As the devils sit in silence and fear as they consider the hazardous, lonely journey, Satan rises, on cue, to assert his "highest worth." In lines echoing the *Aeneid* (6.126–29), Satan uses a false dichotomy, wondering who will undertake the frightening perils of passing through the burning gates of Hell and into the nothingness of Chaos while aware that he alone will venture on such a voyage. He asserts that it is the duty of leadership to undertake such unique, "heroic" action. Since the dangerous journey or quest is a typical means of testing the epic hero, Milton's emphasis on Satan as the antihero, who claims that his high office requires him to act honorably, is clear. The arrogance of this speech ironically contrasts with Messiah's humble acceptance of his mission in the Heavenly Council (3.236–38). Satan, a mock-redeemer seeking Hell's deliverance, silences any response (467), for his glory would be diminished if others were to accompany him. His false promise to deliver his legions reveals that he is not "Sufficient" (404) as a hero, for his bravery, as Book 6 reveals, is the negative counterpart to the selfless heroism of the Son. The false fortitude of the rebel angels is presented, in contrast to Milton's ideal of spiritual fortitude, in terms of useless physical strength and forced, self-serving valor.

With the Council ended, a band of fiery seraphim encircle Hell's emperor, a parody of God's being encircled by the highest choir of angels. After loudly proclaiming the decision of the Council through the vast abyss of Hell, the groups disband, trying to occupy their "restless thoughts" until Satan returns. The sports of the demons remind the reader of the epic games in Homer (*Iliad,* 23) and Virgil (*Aeneid,* 5). Some sing of their "own Heroic deeds" while others ironically indulge in philosophical discussions of "Fate, Free will, Foreknowledge" and, failing to agree, end in humanlike confusion. Milton describes the vain intellectual exercises of the demons who, in "wandering mazes lost," are beyond the pursuit of true virtue and in a state of desperation. Their desire for spiritual strength is a "pleasing sorcery," and their folly is conveyed in strong, physical terms to emphasize their hopeless quest for an external source of strength. Such patience is "stubborn" since it is proud and rigid, the antithesis of true patience, an important Miltonic theme signifying hope and a readiness to accept adversities in order to perfect and mature one's faith.

Other demons, searching for more comfortable quarters, explore Hell in four directions, following the classical rivers of Virgil's underworld (*Aeneid,* 6) that tend to make Hell seem more familiar. The uncertain terrain of Milton's Hell suggests the irrational confusion of the demonic world, represented by the specious debate just concluded.[22] Beyond Lethe (forgetfulness), the fifth river, for example, lies a region where frost and fire paradoxically coexist. As the antithesis of our world, Hell was created evil, Milton says, "for evil only good," emphasizing the paradox with wordplay and with such phrases as "Where all life dies, death lives"; since what God created is good, evil (which God did not create) can only exist in a placeless place of uncreation, perversion, and meaningless negativity, more unnatural, the poet says, than earlier renderings have tried to depict.

Satan's exploratory flight is then compared to the sailing of trading ships in the Indian Ocean, an exotic, remote allusion made more immediate by the reference to contemporary merchants with their "spicy Drugs." Such images are also a positive counterpart to Satan's destructive actions. Satan suddenly faces Hell's nine gates and the symbolic figure of Sin. This begins Milton's only allegorical scene in *Paradise Lost,* an episode indebted to Spenser's Error (*The Faerie Queene,* I.1) and to Ovid's description of Scylla, the nymph transformed by Circe into a mass of yelping hounds from the waist downward (*Metamorphoses,* 14). In one of Milton's richest and most memorable descriptions, more horrible than any visual rendering, the insubstantial shapes of Sin and Death are seated before the "thrice three-fold" gates, indicating an infernal parody of the Trinity, as lines 727–30 make more clear. As elsewhere in the poem, Hell inverts heavenly values.

Satan, unafraid of anyone but God, contemptuously tells the monstrous shapes not to contend with a heavenly spirit. But crowned Death sees through this phony claim, recognizing Satan as the outcast conspirator he is and, aiming his dart at Satan, grows ten times more deadly. Satan, in turn, though thus ridiculed, stands firm and blazes like a comet. The strength of the characters, reflected in their size, and the suspense of this confrontation, intensified by the imagery of cosmic storms, are unique, Milton says, except for the battle between Christ and Satan (721–22) at the end of time.

Sin, interposing herself between the two combatants, addresses Satan as "Father" and Death as "Son" in a blasphemous inversion of heavenly language, reminding Satan that he is God's tool and that fighting Him would be counterproductive. To remind Satan who she is, Sin describes her genesis in Heaven when the rebellion (and hence sin) was conceived in Satan's mind, as Athene (Minerva) sprang from the head of Zeus and as the Son proceeds from the Father. Seeing in her his own "perfect image," a foreshadowing of Eve's glimpse of herself in the reflecting pool (4.456–66), Satan had incest with his "fair" daughter in a metaphorical union between the self and the image of the self. She sprang goddesslike from Satan's left side, as Eve comes from Adam's rib. Death, their offspring, continues to breed incestuously with his mother in a lustful engendering of an endless progeny of evil that Death cannot destroy. She calls Death Satan's "own begotten" offspring and explains that the key of Hell was given to her as the war in Heaven ended.

Like a politician suddenly reminded of new supporters, Satan quickly turns polite in a "smooth" response to the foul figures, claiming that he comes to liberate them. He pictures himself as a lone adventurer, seeming to rival those epic heroes whose dangerous exploits ennoble them. Sin eagerly accepts Satan's false promises and, in lines (864–70) that allude to the heavenly trinity, imagines that she, the demonic counterpart of the Son in glory, will sit at Satan's right hand. The diabolical interaction is a perverse caricature of the divine family.

Slowly, as if reluctant to describe the scene, Milton pictures Sin unlocking "with ease" the massive gates of Hell, which she cannot shut. Chaos, defined negatively as the dimensionless absence of order, appears suddenly as a limitless "Ocean without bound" where embryonic, precreated "Atoms" swirl in a conflict prefiguring the war between good and evil. Chaos is the realm from which all creation rises as a place for God's creative goodness ("The Womb of nature") and as a destructive force ("perhaps her Grave"). Chaos is not inherently good or evil but potentially both: From God's point of view, it is an uncreated state, a part of His being from which He has withdrawn His influence. For Satan, it is the potential source of evil where God's creatures can be ruined, yet destruction always implies its opposite; the Redemption means that the gates of Hell will not prevail. The ambivalence of Chaos is expressed by the male-female personification, Milton implying that through God's influence, the union of these two negative forces will result in the birth of the positive, just as out of evil and disorder will eventually come good and order.

Standing on the "brink of Hell" and looking at this unimaginable nothingness (the image suggesting vertigo), Satan, considering his voyage into this abyss, hears a cosmic roar before he tries to fly in the nonatmosphere. In a microcosm of his earlier fall, he tries vainly to ascend until he drops ten thousand fathoms, rescued only by a clap of thunder that hurls him onto the desert of

Fig. 2. William Blake (1751–1827), *Satan, Sin, and Death*. Reproduced with permission of the Henry E. Huntington Library and Art Gallery.

Chaos. He hears a deafening roar before reaching the throne of Chaos and his "Consort," Night, in a description recalling Spenser's Demogorgon (*The Faerie Queene,* 4) as well as Virgil's palace of Pluto (*Aeneid,* 6). With some anxiety (975), he politely asks the personified figure for directions, assuring him that he comes not to spy, explore, or disturb this realm but hinting nevertheless at "some other place" stolen by God that he might restore to Chaos.

Perhaps this gives Chaos the clue, for he recognizes Satan and provides another (eyewitness) account of the angelic fall before giving Satan his first account of "another World" hanging by a golden chain beyond the frontierless "Frontiers" of Chaos. The governor of this ungovernable vacuity is eager to aid Satan since, he says, Hell and Earth now encroach on his domain.

Satan flies off amid "fighting elements," a course more difficult than that of Jason and the Argonauts, the poet says, or of Ulysses. Behind him Sin and Death build a great bridge (described more fully in Book 10.293–324) so that the devils can pass through Chaos from Hell to "this frail World" in tempting mankind. As he stands at the outermost reaches of the created world, we see the distant light of Heaven through Satan's eyes as he takes in the vast panorama of space, including our entire universe. Such scenes show that the poem is conceived on a tremendous scale, with a modern sense of an immeasurable space beyond the Earth. The poet was influenced by the then-new astronomy of Galileo and Copernicus. *Paradise Lost* is, as a result, "the first modern cosmic poem, in which a drama is played against a background of interstellar space."[23]

## Book 3

The second invocation of the epic (1–55) signals a structural shift from the first two books with their themes of loss and hate to themes of recovery and love in Books 3 and 4. With Book 3, the scene shifts from hellish darkness to the Heavenly realm where "God is Light." There Milton introduces his notion of God's perfection, which is changeless, unlike created perfection, which can change as required by free choice. The invocation also shows Milton's awareness of the differing types of vision, the purposes of sight, and the ways in which physical and mental eyes perceive.

With these interrelated themes of light, vision, and perfection, the poet-narrator moves up from Hell's "utter darkness" through the "middle darkness" of Chaos, with Satan perched on the edge of the world to glimpse a distant celestial light, and then to this welcome ascent to Heaven, where, newly inspired, Milton will tell of "things invisible to mortal sight." The blind poet, who can only see by hearing, prays for spiritual insight so that, like Homer and Tiresias, he can see with the inner eye of the mind. The Fall will produce the reverse pattern: vision leads to sin, darkening and closing the eyes of the mind.

In his prayer Milton worships God, who said "Let there be light" (Genesis 1.3) and who is identified with light (1 John 1.5). Milton, always concerned with light as a sacred, supernatural mystery, here conceives of the Son as combining the uncreated light of God with the created light ("offspring") that reflects God's eternal radiance.[24] That this Godhead is unknowable, unnamable, and indescribable is apparent from the poet's mysteriously worded refusal to name the nature of God: "bright effluence of bright essence." That is, God is an approachable fountain of uncreated, eternal brightness that human sight can never penetrate. If man is in inevitable darkness, blinded by God's mysterious light, the poet's physical blindness prompts an emphasis on the need for inner vision in movingly personal terms that recall Sonnet 19 and *Samson Agonistes*. Like Adam's at the end of *Paradise Lost,* the poet's spiritual vision must be strengthened, along with the reader's imaginative vision, so that the narrator can "see and tell" future events.

The emphasis on vision continues: the angel hosts receive unutterable bliss from seeing God, whose all-seeing eye bends down to encompass in one view all His works. He sees "our two first Parents" in prelapsarian innocence as well as Satan coasting along the boundary of Heaven. Milton then proceeds from God's view of events in time to a timeless foreseeing in which God speaks in an imageless, anonymous, authoritative voice. In this state of immutable perfection, the reader can see nothing, hearing only the absolute Word. God's truths, Milton suggests, must be voiced in a simplicity that is largely barren of ornament. As God is the antithesis of Satan, so his utterances are devoid of flourishes and elaboration. He speaks without fanfare and theatricality. The plainer style of these speeches calls into question the rhetorical grandeur of Books 1 and 2. The style of Satan, Stanley Fish notes, is digressive, moving away from logical coherence and calling attention to the virtuosity of the speaker; God's style is austere, to the point, with a minimal intrusion of personality and of figures of speech; as a result, there is little sense of style apart from thought.[25]

As He speaks to the Son, the expression of His glory, the Father sees past, present, and future at once and so uses tenses interchangeably. Considering what Satan will do to man, God angrily calls the future race of man ungrateful and disloyal since man was created "right": "Sufficient to have stood, though free to fall" (99). This line applies to both angels and men and is part of an important theological passage in which man's view of God and human freedom is the central and related issues. As Rajan notes, Adam is not meant to complete himself *in* Eve but *with* her, the two enriching each other as they reflect God's perfection. Eve is made strong enough, or sufficient, to stand with Adam; she becomes insufficient when she deems herself independent and more than sufficient.[26] Human freedom is thus defined as the cause of the Fall of man, who, God says, has no one to blame but himself. Good and bad angels were created with free will, which is necessary if they are to demonstrate their love for and obedience to their Creator, a forced reverence being a contradiction. The Fall depends on the volition of man and angels; God's foreknowledge is not responsible. He cannot bestow free will and reason and then prevent their use. God outlines the doctrine of foreknowledge, which, Milton wrote in *Christian Doctrine*, has "no connection with the principle or essence of predestination." What God knows outside of time is not an action with an "influence" (118) that could affect moral choice. Thus all rational creatures are "Authors" of their own destinies and can only lose freedom by discarding it. The link between human and angelic creatures stressed here recalls the poet's emphasis on the developing parallel between the fall of the angels and the downfall of humankind, especially at this juncture of the poem when the focus will shift from Hell to Earth. The rebellious angels were "self-tempted" (130), whereas man will fall "deceiv'd" by Satan and thus will deserve grace. The Deity uses repetition of ideas and words (*fall, fell, fault, fail'd*) to emphasize doctrine as well as to deride the folly of His creatures.

The Father's address to the Son, if looked at dramatically, seems wooden and contrived, with the Son as the clear subordinate. If looked at metaphorically, the vexing question of the Son's equality with the Father seems less important. The Son, who speaks the thoughts of the Father, expresses His love and mercy, which are inseparable from the justice that both Persons (manifestations) of the Trinity share with the Holy Spirit. It is as if the "dialogue" is within the mind of one being. The relation between Father and Son reflects Milton's unorthodox view (in *Christian Doctrine*) that the Father is greater than the Son, though the poem asserts that the two are one (169–70). If Milton refuses to acknowledge the equality of the three Persons within the Godhead, he accepts the participation of Son and Spirit in the substance of the Father. The mystery of the Trinity is important in understanding man's relation to God in terms of creation (Father), redemption (Son), and enlightenment (Spirit).

Heaven joins the Son in rejoicing at the news of divine mercy for man and of Satan's ultimate defeat. The Father then explains his "Eternal purpose," which requires atonement, so that the mercy of God is seen in the Father as well as in the Son. "Man must be saved out of love and mercy: man must also be saved lest evil go unpunished and justice be betrayed."[27] In lines that seem to uphold a strict Calvinist interpretation of absolute predestination (183–90), Milton's God, in fact, rejects such a doctrine, proclaiming that some men have been chosen for special grace above unbelievers ("the rest") but that salvation is available to all believers, who are promised enlightenment and the inner guidance of conscience. Milton never insists, as does Calvin, that those not receiving grace will be damned but that salvation will come to all who choose to obey, pray, and repent. They have grace because they believe.

The Heavenly Council parallels its hellish counterpart (Book 2) as angelic choirs stand in suspenseful silence until the Son offers to take on the humiliation of becoming human to intercede for man. The Father's love is reflected in the Son with such "fullness" that judgment alone without mercy and love is seen as impossible. Milton explains that divine grace is freely given, an unsought gift, necessitated by man's sin. The Son says that man, unable to find help on his own, needs external aid (234). The Son's repeated emphasis on "Mee" (236–38), is a humbly sincere contrast to the egocentrism of Satan in the hellish Council. Milton explains the doctrine (246–51) that God will die for man *in* the flesh but not *with* the flesh since the Son's divinity is alien to death, over which He will "rise Victorious." The Father then articulates the doctrine of the Incarnation: since no one but God could satisfy God in atoning for man's sin, the redemption must be undertaken by God's becoming man and standing in Adam's place (the Second Adam). The Redeemer's death will mean life, and the Son of Man will ransom the human race, replacing "Hellish hate" with love; this is made clear in the Father's important announcement that the Son's humiliation "shall exalt" (313): The Son will strip Himself of his divinity to redeem man, raising him from sin before reascending to the Father's right hand. What Satan falsely promises in Books 1 and 2, the Son actually achieves for mankind through His death and resurrection; and by descending into Hell, He releases souls from captivity and thus offers salvation to all. As the Father makes clear (305–11), the Son's willingness to put aside the Godhead does not entail a loss of divinity. The kingship of the Son, following his crucifixion, will make possible fallen man's ascent to his "blissful Seat" (1.5).

As the angels rejoice at the Son's exaltation, Heaven is seen as richly jeweled (as in Revelation 4) and filled with harmonious rapture. God is worshiped by angelic hosts crowned with gold and "Immortal Amarant," the deathless flower that grew in Heaven, the poet says, before being planted in Eden by the Tree of Life; after the Fall, it was returned to Heaven. This revealing analogy between Heaven and its reflection, Earth, also encapsulates the descent-ascent pattern of the Son in leaving eternal perfection for earthly imperfection before being restored to Heaven. The angels then sing a hymn of praise to the Son, to which Milton adds a personal address (410–15) to the Savior, whose love for man constitutes the truest heroism.

Satan, walking alone on the outermost sphere of the universe, returns the reader to the more familiar vocabulary of vision, similes, and geographical references. The world (or universe) is seen as a vast wasteland where the enemy of mankind is "bent" (*inclined* as well as *crooked*) on his prey. Milton pauses to explain that this grim vacuity on the outside surface of the world will become a Limbo of Vanity or Paradise of Fools, to be filled by what is *vain*, a word repeated for its mocking effect. This comic episode (444–97) on the "backside of the world" is not so much a digression as a transition between Heaven and Earth where the epic bard can attack pretension and folly. He lists those who, trying to achieve illusory fame or happiness on earth, will throw away their chance for salvation and float up to this place because of their vaporous emptiness, a place where freaks and fanatics join friars, pilgrims, and other representations of Milton's anti-Catholic attack on superstition. Blown by violent winds, they pass by the planets to the primum mobile or outermost sphere (483), where Satan now stands. Drawn by a distant gleam of light, he hastens to the magnificent gates of Heaven, where he sees a stairway that Milton ironically compares to the ladder on which Jacob saw angels ascending and descending (Genesis 18.12). The poet is providing us with another example of the Christ-Satan polarity in the poem: Since the ladder of Jacob was often seen as prefiguring the Redemption and Resurrection, the poet can again suggest that what Satan tries to promise—liberation and ascent—Christ actually achieves.

The poet says that sometimes the stairs are let down, a mystery leading to another mystery: are the stairs let down to tempt the fiend to enter Heaven or to remind him of his banishment? The base of the stairs leads down to Earth so that unfallen man and God can pass easily to and fro. With God presumably at the summit of the heavenly stairs, Satan, his antithesis, stands "on the lower stair" where he views the universe in one glance "with wonder," as when a "Scout" catches a sudden glimpse of a glittering city at dawn. Satan's envy at the sight of our world is meant as a compliment to our world, which God has created and will enter in order to redeem. Flying down through the smooth, shining ("marble") air, he sees the panorama of the stars, then plunges through the upper air ("World's first Region"), through the orbs of the primum mobile, the Crystalline Sphere, and the fixed stars; entering the lower region of the planets, he is attracted by the sun (which is "above" the stars in the sense that it is more splendid than they and "dispenses Light" to them).[28] The sun warms the universe by paternal insemination; nature-earth is archetypally conceived as a female principle fertilized by the creative male force.

Seeming to land on the orb of the sun, Satan becomes a solar spot, thereby marring the Godlike source of light, on a surface so radiant it exceeds the radiance of any single earthly metal or stone. The clear air and shadowless noontime light sharpen Satan's vision, which soon identifies an angel (as in Revelation 19.17). Satan quickly appears as a guardian angel, dressed in a gaudy costume of curly, flowing hair and colored wings sprinkled with gold. Yet the trick works: Satan's first disguise deceives Uriel,* who as Regent of the Sun, has the keenest angelic eye. The lesson is clear for the reader: If this archangel can be deceived, man's seduction by a fallen archangel will not be surprising. Satan's request for heavenly guidance ironically inverts Milton's invocation to light; the fiend pretends that he wishes to visit and admire God's new creature and, by implication, the Creator. Milton explains that only God can penetrate hypocrisy, which is made possible because of His permissive will, and that the angels are not suspicious of fraud. Uriel sees Satan as a "Fair Angel" and sings God's praises. He briefly recounts the story of creation, to which he was an eyewitness, before pointing out earth. There, full of hope for success, he flies off.

## Book 4

Milton's epic voice, which varies from that of moralist to satirist to symbolic everyman, is also personal and prophetic, as in the opening of the fourth book. As Satan approaches the Earth, the narrator's tone is one of lament and regret that "our first Parents," soon to be introduced, were not warned of their "secret foe." The repeated assonance (*now, down,* etc.) enhances this tone and the speaker's sense of pathos since the inevitable Fall will change human existence for the worse, though the ultimate outcome will be spiritually fortunate. He longs for a voice such as John the evangelist heard (in Revelation 12.10) in his prophecy of Satan's defeat at the end of time; thus Milton sets the story of Eden, which now begins, in the wide sweep of history, foreseeing its ultimately happy resolution.

*Though not cited in the Bible, Uriel was one of the great archangels of Jewish tradition who ruled the four quarters of the world. The others were Michael, known to Christians as the warrior angel who is to battle the Dragon of the Apocalypse (Revelation 12.7–9); Raphael, familiar to Milton's readers from the Book of Tobit as a heavenly protector and deliverer; and Gabriel (Daniel 8.16 and Luke 1.36–38), best known as the messenger of God who announced to Mary the news of Jesus' birth.

Arriving in noon's fullest light, Satan is tormented by the Hell "within him" as he jealously views man's happy abode. Aware of the difference between good and evil, he considers what he is, what he has lost, and what he is about to do. Addressing the sun, which reminds him of God and of his own lost glory, he vents his rage since he knows he is forever condemned to darkness; he reveals not only the full dimension of his hate but also his somewhat more "honest" sense of sin and guilt. "Ah wherefore!" (42), "Me miserable!" (73), and "Ay me" (86) are laments foreign to the Satan of Books 1 and 2. In spelling out the consequences of his still-obvious pride (49–51), he seems tragically human, acknowledging that God, who gave him his brilliance, deserved only praise and thanks. Without his former rhetorical flourishes, he condemns and curses himself, but his newly revealed self-knowledge contains no redemptive hope: "Which way I fly is Hell; myself am Hell." These lines recall the preposterous boast, "The mind is its own place, and in itself / Can make a Heav'n of Hell, a Hell of Heav'n" (1.255). He now knows that he cannot turn Hell into Heaven by wishful thinking, but he has been able to convert part of Heaven into Hell by the force of his tormented mind.

Milton, ever interested in the psychology of evil, portrays an escapist who cannot escape himself, who curses himself for choosing what he now regrets. The point is not to create sympathy for the devil but to show the workings of despair, the mental anguish of a soul lost, without hope of salvation, in the agonized conflicts of his own mind, which Satan prefers to the reality of the outside world. In raising the futile possibility of repentance, Satan, like Marlowe's Dr. Faustus, continually runs into the barrier of his own pride ("Disdain forbids me") and the maze of what might have been. He concedes that, even if repentance were possible, he would revolt again and his submission thus would be "feign'd" (96). He grandly says farewell to hope and remorse, while bitterly grieving, and is forced to accept evil as his only good, though less cheerfully than when he bade farewell to Heaven and greeted the horrors of Hell in Book 1. He remains deceived in thinking that he now controls "more than half" of God's "Divided Empire." The degeneration of Satan has begun: in his single-minded determination to destroy mankind, he becomes less and less interesting as a character. If his humanization makes him more understandable, it also reflects his weakness as compared with man; he is the adversary of man, not, as he has claimed, of God.

Eden, which contains a paradise (walled garden), and the surrounding wilderness are seen through Satan's eyes, suggesting that nothing earthly, not even Eden, is secure from evil. Its beauty and scents nearly intoxicate Satan, who is revealingly compared to one sailing "Beyond the Cape of Hope" since the landscape momentarily drives away demonic sadness but not despair. Soon he leaps over the boundary like a "prowling Wolf" into a sheepfold, symbolic of the church. He is then compared to a thief climbing into a rich man's well-secured house, a contemporary image that Milton uses to warn the reader of human vulnerability. Satan perches on the tree of immortality where, like a greedy, diving cormorant, he ironically plots the death of humankind while wondering at the sight of nature's richness. As the garden is magnified and made geographically real (as for example, by the place names of lines 211–14), animal images deflate the once-splendid picture of Satan provided in Books 1 and 2.

In describing the garden in Eden, Milton considerably expands the Genesis account: "And out of the ground made the Lord God to grow every tree that is pleasant to the sight, and good for food; the tree of life also in the midst of the garden, and the tree of knowledge of good and evil." Milton's Eden, the positive counterpart to Hell, has four main rivers, whose "wand'ring" suggests the future of man after the Fall. Since Earth is a reflection of Heaven, the poet uses some of the same jeweled imagery (237–38) as he does in describing, or seeming to describe, Heaven. Like Heaven, Eden is a place of great abundance and unimaginable riches; it is beyond time and change, with an ordered, harmonious cycle of day and night, work and rest, as dictated by nature and sanctified by God. It is significant that Satan comes to Eden in the evening, the time of repose, intimacy, and greatest security, when Adam and Eve are most vulnerable; the same time is used when Satan stirs up his rebellion in Heaven in Book 5 (653). The descriptions of the day and nature add to the sense of the innocence and bliss in the garden and of its inhabitants. Their repose resembles heavenly peace and contrasts with the restless, changeless state of the demons in Hell.

The beauty of the flowers, the murmuring waters, the lush vines, and the air that stirs the leaves in a melodic breeze convey the goodness in this garden, which Milton contrasts with lesser, mythological bowers (268–83). But it is not a perfect pastoral place free of tensions; it is, rather, a moral testing ground. Man's innocence in Eden is conditional, not effortless, Milton repeatedly shows us; the earthly paradise does not produce stability but requires vigilance in the form of temperance. Excessive growth must be controlled. The forbidden fruit is not the only source of restraint in Eden: Adam and Eve must learn to keep aspiration within natural limits to maintain their place on the Chain of Being. The inhabitants of Eden are seen in Books 4 and 5 as gardeners responsible for ordering nature. They have been planted by God, to grow and be cultivated, perfecting their own natures. They, like the garden, are not static but share in the ongoing process of creative nature.

The first view of Adam and Eve, who "seem'd" lords of nature, contains the same sense that perfection is conditional, requiring ongoing effort, self-denial, and obedience. Eve's hair is "disshev-ell'd" (loose and free) and "wanton" (curled), yet these words have an inescapably postlapsarian connotation. Milton's purpose is to describe unimaginable human innocence in terms of our fallen world and to foreshadow the Fall.

The poet adds a few details to the generalized picture of mankind's progenitors, viewed from Satan's perspective. They are seen as erect or rational, superior to the beasts, for the human pair bears God's image (291–92). Adam's "Hyacinthine Locks" suggest a "superhuman beauty such as Athene (in the *Odyssey*, 6) gave to Ulysses when she made him taller and mightier than ordinary men and gave him flowing locks like the hyacinth flower." [29] Clearly they are different and unequal: "Hee for God only, she for God in him," reflecting the traditional view that the image of God is more perfectly reflected in the man than in the woman, who is the image of man. Yet the woman's independent spirit in submitting to her husband is beautifully conveyed in 310–11: she "Yielded with coy submission, modest pride / And sweet reluctant amorous delay." As symbolic, complementary figures of ideal human nature, they are both lords of creation as well as God's subjects; much as the Son expresses the Father's love and mercy in the heavenly family, so also Eve theologically expresses the passive, obedient nature of Adam with whom she is linked in an inseparable union.

The poet's recurring emphasis on Adam and Eve's unashamed nudity, symbolizing their unfallen innocence and the goodness of God's creation, contrasts with the lustful state of fallen sexuality and reveals that marriage and sexual relations are a major theme of the poem. As they recline on flowers and enjoy the tame animals (335–50), Adam and Eve are in perfect harmony with nature, which is always easily within reach, and which also includes the "smiles" and love-play of a happily married couple lacking nothing. Eve, adorned in "Naked beauty," also recalls the biblical vision of the new Jerusalem prepared as a bride adorned for her husband (Revelation 21.3), thus pointing up the correspondence between earthly and heavenly kingdoms.

Satan, watching them with envy and hate since he sees that they are made in God's likeness, feels an impulse to pity Adam and Eve, though he is beyond God's pity. His admiration intensifies his eagerness to destroy them, and he seeks his own "mutual amity" with them so that, he says, they will dwell with him, imagining Hell opening wide its gates to receive their "numerous offspring." Satan is so degenerate that he is blind to any truth: if he is unable to offer Adam and Eve a better dwelling, he says to himself, they can blame God. Though claiming to be moved by their "harmless innocence," he says that the common good ("public reason just") forces him to seek what is, in fact, chosen personal vengeance.

Trying to come closer and learn more, Satan assumes various animal shapes. Thus disguised as a predator, he listens to Adam in his first speech tell Eve that God's unmerited goodness deserves obedience, including compliance with the arbitrary edict against eating of the tree of knowledge. Though ignorant of what the penalty—death—might be, Adam concludes that, given their wide freedom, one such command is easily honored. Eve then recalls her first moment of self-awareness in dreamlike terms. With an implied analogy to the Narcissus legend, Milton has her explain in wondrous words how she gazed lovingly at her own image in a smooth lake that seemed like the heavenly sky inverted, a revealing suggestion of a sinlike reversal: her vanity looks forward to the later sin of pride. But she says that God's voice telling her that the beautiful reflection was of herself prevented "vain desire." When she first saw Adam, she found him "less fair" than her own reflected image and turned from him, foreshadowing their future separation and sin, just as the emphasis on vision in her speech prefigures the temptation in Book 9, where Satan promises that her eyes will be opened. Adam had told her that she was created from his body (Genesis 2.23); now she sees, somewhat reluctantly, that manly grace excels female beauty. Thus the reader is aware that Eve's unfallen womanhood not only contains the seeds of sin but an uncertainty about what beauty truly is. Though she yields to her husband's natural superiority, Eve is already perceived as having the potential for sin, as her later dream (5.673–74) more clearly reveals.

Satan turns away in envy from the couple "Imparadis't in one another's arms" and develops his plot, based on having heard Adam speak of the forbidden tree. Satan pretends that God has foolishly denied access to the Tree of Knowledge of Good and Evil and that man's happy state is based on ignorance. Maliciously distorting what we have also heard from Adam, Satan gleefully concludes that he has a "fair" foundation on which to devise his destructive plan. He will use God's law, which he sees as a means to keep Adam and Eve "low," to bring about their downfall by playing upon the very aspiration that ruined Satan himself.

Meanwhile, at the eastern gate of paradise, on a towering rock, sits Gabriel with other angelic guards. The guardian of paradise and of Adam is significantly the same angel who will announce to Mary (Luke 1.26) the good news of the second Adam. Warned by Uriel that the spirit he had directed to Eden (Satan) is on his way, Gabriel says that no physical barrier can exclude the entrance of "one of the banish't crew." As Uriel returns to the sphere of the sun and evening descends, Adam and Eve retire. Adam speaks of the ordered cycle of nature that dictates rest as well as work: branches are "overgrown" and require pruning lest Eden become "unsightly," as if the pleasant labor of maintaining God's creation already requires "more hands" (629), a foreshadowing of the separation of the couple in Book 9.

Eve's response indicates her joy in being with Adam and in obeying God's law through him: "God is thy Law, thou mine." Love and obedience for Milton are inseparable, part of the hierarchy in which nature, including mankind, reflects God's order and by which man can ascend to God. Reflecting the idea that happiness is obeying the order of nature, she praises the solemn beauty of "this delightful Land" in a lovely hymnlike description (641–56) of their world. As Harry Blamires says, the mutuality of Adam and Eve reflects the divine union of Father and Son, parodied by the infernal trinity. Adam's addressing Eve as "Daughter of God and Man" recalls the Son "both of God and Man" (3.316). "If there seems to be a relationship of sovereignty and obedience between man and woman, it is not more remarkable than that between Father and Son."[30]

Having explained that everything in nature has a purpose, Adam walks with Eve "hand in hand" to their private, flower-bedecked bower, which defies the poet's efforts to describe it. The lush carpet of flowers on which they lie is more colorful than stone inlaid with precious metal, the poet says, and classical bowers (705–8) cannot match this paradise within a paradise sanctified by their love. Eve in her naked beauty is seen as more beautiful that the primal woman of Greek myth, Pandora, whose marriage to Prometheus' brother unleashed evils on mankind, a revealing classical analogue to Eve's future sin. The poet maintains the unashamed sexual intercourse of Adam and Eve (often denied by earlier theologians who, associating sin with sex, insisted that they had sexual relations only after the Fall) to signify that such unfallen pleasure, far from being evil, reflects a natural, holy union. The poet not only defends prelapsarian sexuality but sings the praises of "wedded Love," personally contrasting it with the lust of harlots and the artificial court revelries of Restoration London.

Gabriel orders an angelic night patrol to watch the borders of the garden, and Ithuriel and Zephon, two archangels, look for Satan, whom they find close to Eve's ear, "Squat like a toad," in the most private, secure part of the garden. As she sleeps, the devil is trying to reach her imagination ("Fancy") to create dreams and illusions, "vain hopes, vain aims, inordinate desires," or to taint her blood (801–9). Milton's use of "Or" complicates the reader's understanding of the fiend's action, which results in Eve's dream (5.28–93), and the dream is significant for its relation to her later sinfulness. If Satan causes her dream, she is not responsible for it; but if the dream reflects her tainted blood, she is seen to be corrupt before the Fall. But what she says in Book 5 about her dream confirms the former possibility, not the latter: that Satan has success only in working on her imagination. If Eve were weakened by Satan here, her failure to reject his tempting words in Book 9 would be a preconditioned act rather than a sin, which is a conscious turning from God; and God's justice would be questioned. Thus one must conclude that Eve remains free to choose and that her later dream, apparently influenced by Satan, does not signify her guilt but his responsibility. This episode, interestingly preparing for the main temptation in Book 9, requires one to judge the innocence of the couple and the guile of the tempter; as a result, the reader responds to the Fall itself with greater sympathy.

The reader, unaware of the possible consequences of Satan's "Devilish art," is relieved that the angels catch the fiend in the act of trying to penetrate Eve's mind. Flaring up like a spark of gunpowder, he surprises the angels by instantly resuming his "own shape." Unable to pull rank, Satan nevertheless tries to ridicule the angels for not recognizing him, to which Zephon replies that Satan's glory is departed. Standing abashed, Satan realizes how wonderful goodness is, how beautiful angels are, and thus how great his loss is.

Satan, having ridiculed Ithuriel and Zephon, is led to the western end of the garden where Gabriel, recognizing his "faded splendor," is about to challenge him as dishonest, disloyal, and hypocritical. Satan has transgressed the sacred place of earthly bliss, as he has in Heaven, and has violated the ban on entering Earth. Contemptuous of Gabriel's wisdom, he responds that anyone would try to escape Hell's pains but sees that his explanation is incomprehensible to an unfallen angel. Then, as the angel squadron mocks Satan by surrounding him with their spears, he stands "dilated," his stature enlarged by summoning up his strength, so that he seems like a mountain peak. War would have ensued, the poet explains, had not God prevented it. The symbolic scales of divine justice reveal to Satan that flight outweighs fighting since the good angels receive their strength from God, whose will is that good and evil remain balanced until the end of time. Seeing his fortune in his scale, which has flown upward, he flees.

## Book 5

Having been introduced to the main characters and locales in the first four swiftly moving books, the reader is given a slower middle section of suspended action, narrative history, and flashback in Books 5–8, consisting of the education of Adam. As the reader receives needed background, Adam learns about good and evil, choice and obedience so that his upcoming sin is not committed in ignorance. Since the reader knows the outcome of the story, Milton had to emphasize why Adam and Eve fell. As the poet's prefatory argument states, the action of Book 1 hastens "into the midst of things" (in medias res), passing over Satan's revolt in Heaven and the ensuing action of man's creation. Hence the structural and thematic need for Books 5–8: they prepare for Adam's loss of paradise by a flashback to the heavenly war and the story of Creation while developing the motivation by which man could sin. Adam must learn about Nature and human nature. As George Williamson says, the education of Adam is part of the poet's epic strategy: "The didactic element is intended both to motivate and to amplify the tragic consequences of the fall of man."[31]

Adam is awakened by the sound of leaves stirred by the goddess of morning, Aurora, and by the song of birds. By contrast, Eve, still sleeping, appears restless and out of harmony with the beauties of nature. In words derived from the Song of Solomon, Adam whispers an erotic aubade (dawn song) that suggests his desire to worship Eve rather than God. She awakes, startled and relieved to see her husband after a troubling dream prompted by Satan, who, we recall from 4.800, had been squatting like a toad by her ear. In her dream, she hears a voice that she mistakes for Adam's praise the moonlight as more fair than the sunlight. Unaware that Satan has imitated Adam's love song, she is awed by the suggestion that the night is exciting and that nature is ready to admire her beauty. Flattery thus compounds her inclination to vanity. Failing to find Adam, she comes to the forbidden tree of knowledge, which appears lovelier in the night of the dream than in the light of reality. She sees an angelic figure who praises the tree in words that prepare for the temptation scene of Book 9 (498–833). Eve's vanity, as in Book 4 (449–91), and sense of amazement render her helpless in coping with Satan's suggestion that the prohibition is unreasonable. Shocked to see him eat, she nevertheless falls for the tempter's promise of greater wisdom and happiness if she will rise above her earthly station and become one of the gods, as he claims to have done. Unable to resist the sweet-smelling fruit, all the more alluring because forbidden, the dreamer eats and ascends with the angel-like deceiver, only to find herself finally alone.

This dream, Eve's first experience with temptation, anticipates her fall. Still, she remains the innocent victim of Satan, who is now poised to taint the unfallen world. The dream also foreshadows Adam's sin, for he, too, will turn from God to Eve as she turns from Adam to Satan. Though this dream may be interpreted psychologically as a wish fulfillment (for power or as a rebellion against Adam's dominance), it occurs in an unfallen world and is caused by an external agent. Milton, while depicting the beginnings of the unconscious mind, uses the dream as prophecy and poetic foreshadowing. Adam cannot be expected to see it as a warning or to know that Satan has succeeded in reaching Eve's "Fancy," forging "Illusions." Instead of reminding Eve to obey God's law, he gives a lecture on the soul's faculties that cause phantasms. He is certain that evil cannot reside in Eve, who is part of him; evil can pass harmlessly, he says, through the mind since creation includes the potential for evil in what is good. Thus he states his innocent conviction that what Eve did "abhor" to do in the dream she will never do in fact. Kissing away her tears, Adam leads her into the morning light, in contrast to the darkness praised in the dream; there, in a landscape connoting order and well-being, they praise God with unrehearsed, spontaneous eloquence. This prayer reflects Milton's belief that all creation is good, coming from God.

Calmed by their prayer, they hasten to return to their work. Milton views life in the garden as difficult and fraught with danger. The abundance of the garden indicates not only God's bountiful goodness but also the need for human temperance. They are able to train the vine's "marriageable arms" as it encircles the elm but will be less disciplined in their own marriage. As God beholds Adam and Eve in their garden, He also sees Satan already at work on the human pair and calls Raphael to warn them of their conditionally happy state: their happiness is due to their free, changeable will. Divine justice requires that man be told that he will be led astray "by deceit and wiles" lest he be surprised. Since Eden is a moral testing ground for archetypal human nature, the specific nature of the deceit is not revealed.

Passing to the gate of Heaven, Raphael sees Earth and Eden more keenly than any earthly astronomer. Flying down at once with more certainty than Satan displayed in his similar flight (3.528–87) and with more grace than Mercury's journey in the *Aeneid* (4.241), the six-winged seraph looks to the eagles like the legendary phoenix as he descends to the garden. Like Abraham who saw the Lord coming and told Sarah to prepare a meal, Adam calls Eve to prepare a bountiful dinner to honor the visitor from Heaven, which has so generously provided Eden with nature's gifts. The abundant feast is described with multisensory richness, symbolizing the beauty of Eden and man's participation in heavenly joys.

They enter the flower-covered bower, but Eve is uncovered, Milton emphasizing that her beautiful perfection, greater than that of Juno, Minerva, and Venus, needs no adorning. In words echoing the angelic greeting to Mary (Luke 1.28), Raphael hails Eve as the "Mother of Mankind," whose fruitful womb is reflected in the plenitude of the garden. As they eat, the angel explains that all created things take nourishment. This should tell Adam and Eve something important: that they do not need special food to advance their state, as the serpent will claim. Because the angelic substance differs only in degree from the human since both participate in the divine nature, the angels actually consume food. For Milton this is not a poetic convention; he believed that since angels assume visible shapes, they include all physical as well as rational human faculties; they are higher beings because of their inclusiveness.[32]

Adam, eager not to let the "occasion pass," politely asks Raphael about heavenly beings, inquiring how earthly food could be compared with Heaven's "high feasts." The angel provides an important doctrinal lesson on the hierarchy of being: God created all things from Himself, from matter that is an extension of His being, and matter is constantly being perfected, returning to the Creator. The substances of things are purer the higher they are on the scale of being. The tree analogy (479–90) shows that everything in creation serves its immediate superior in the hierarchy and thereby moves up "to spirit" in symbiotic union; the implication is that, without the Fall, Adam and Eve would be so inseparable from each other and from the rest of creation that they would finally "turn all to spirit" and choose either to dwell in Heaven or in the earthly paradise so long as they remain obedient, a condition Eve will forget. The possibility of man's rising to angelic status is a seed planted in Adam's ear. But he is more eager to understand the possibility of disobedience. The answer is clear: God-given human happiness requires obedience since man was created perfect but "not immutable": that is, perfection contains the possibility of change because of free will. Raphael asserts what Satan contradicts: that God requires chosen, not compulsory, obedience. Enforced service would not be service, he explains, adding that the angels' happiness depends on the same ongoing obedience and love as man's.

Adam is sure that he and Eve will never neglect to love and obey God's sole command but, curious about Raphael's reference to some angels who fell, asks for the full story of how this occurred. Raphael's difficult task in relating the war in Heaven reveals Milton's problem: how to explain in human terms what is not only hidden from man but invisible to the senses. Since Earth is both a Platonic reflection and a foreshadowing ("shadow") of Heaven, the poet and his angelic narrator will use analogy, likening "spiritual to corporal forms." With this as a poetic basis and with the hierarchical theory of being (469–505) in mind, the reader is prepared to go back to the beginning of the story of the epic. The action earlier passed over becomes a lesson in obedience, which for Milton is inseparable from love. Raphael, who counters Satan's proud perversion of love into hate, is the poet's chief spokesman for the virtues one needs for moral education.

Raphael's story begins in Heaven before the world's creation, when the angels were already created, Milton rejecting the more orthodox view that they were created and fell during the Creation. He also attacked the idea that time as the measure of motion could not have existed before the world was made. In specifying one "day" in eternity, the poet relied on Psalm 2.6–7: "Thou art my Son; this day have I begotten thee." Thus the chronological narrative of the epic begins with the exaltation of the Son. God is described with poetic legerdemain as the invisible bright center (in contrast to Satan's "darkness visible") around which thousands of angels stand, circle upon circle, their countless flags and banners streaming, a tableau parodied in Hell (1.544–49). In decreeing that the Son is "begot[ten]" (603), or metaphorically generated, the Father is not saying that the Son's divine nature is being created but exalted, as prophesied in Book 3 (305–22). In the presence of the angels the Son assumes their nature as the manifestation of the Father's lordship. Thus the angelic hosts are to maintain the unity of Heaven by obeying the Son, whose kingship is shared with the Father.

As Albert Labriola points out, Milton uses various scriptural and apocryphal sources to show that the Son is exalted because of his divinity and his willingness to be humiliated. The poet adds the Son's exaltation as an angel to make Satan's revolt against the Son's newly designated kingship more plausible. Satan, then called Lucifer, was the highest ranking angel, whose Godlike status he himself makes clear in Book 1. Thus the Son's kingship and revelation as an angel in Book 5 strike Satan as an outrageous insult. Feeling that he has been deposed, he argues that the other angels have been degraded because they must worship a recently begotten angel. Abdiel will explain that God's intention is to exalt all the angels, not demean them (829–31), for this begetting provides a manifestation of the Deity more similar and understandable to the angelic nature. Satan for the first time must pay homage to a being who shares his nature. What he sees as tyranny Abdiel insists (835) is an elevation of the angels' dignity. Rather than humble himself, Satan seeks to upgrade his previous status as governor of the angels to that of a god, an effort antithetical to the Son's humiliation, just as Satan's later defeat and debasement reverse the Son's movement from humiliation to exaltation.[33]

In contrast to the joyful song of Heaven that pledges obedience to the Son is the picture of Satan, alone awake in the pleasant twilight of Heaven's night, enviously brooding over the Son's newly proclaimed kingship. This is the earliest view of Satan, who is never seen as unfallen in the epic but even now is resolved to leave God's throne "Unworshipt, unobey'd." In a secret conspiracy he awakens Beelezebub, upsetting the tranquil order of Heaven by proposing new consideration of the law of obedience and pretending that they withdraw to prepare a reception for their new king, Messiah. Thus Lucifer, whose name Milton avoids using, draws off "with lies" a third of the angelic host.

God sees the dissension: the Father speaks "smiling" (in sarcasm) to the Son, laughing at the vain schemes of a foe who tries to rival God. If the War in Heaven is seen as a divine comedy in which pure spirits waging physical battles are ridiculous and absurd, the element of mockery is important (see 737). If the Son seems to delight in punishing the proud rebels, the Father clearly enjoys the irony of an angel trying to unseat the omnipotent, eternal maker of all things.

Already Satan and his armies are vast and numberless as they hasten to a high hill, an "imitation" of the hill on which Messiah was exalted. There they hear Satan suggest that the angelic titles have less meaning since the Son has been anointed king. How, he asks, can we endure the double indignity of homage to the Father as well as to his image? His specious logic is subtle: He suggests that since equality is equivalent to freedom, if the angels are not fully equal, they are not free (791–97). Thus no one can impose laws on, or be elevated above, them. Abdiel (literally, Servant of God), a character invented by Milton to embody zeal, sharply rebukes Satan's dishonesty and blasphemy. Abdiel asserts that the Deity has enhanced angelic dignity by making the Son "One of our number."

The challenge increases Satan's confidence as he questions the "strange" new doctrine that the angels were created by the "secondary hands" of the Son, as Abdiel has asserted. Since we cannot remember any state without existence or consciousness, Satan then contends, it must follow that we were "self-begot, self-rais'd." Denying that he is a creature, Satan has tried to prove that he is a self-sufficient being, concocting lies to turn angelic loyalties toward God into resentment. Only Abdiel among Satan's forces remains faithful and obedient; only Abdiel sees that it is too late for argument since Satan has sinned and will be damned.

Satan's hatred and envy of the Son as "anointed King" are at the heart of his proud rebellion and of the subsequent war. As Stella Revard has shown, Milton uses the war in Heaven to show how evil results from a good creature's conscious mischoice. Adam's perception of God's ways and the reader's understanding of Milton's theology require a comprehension of why Satan not only failed but refused to obey. Seeing obedience to God as an irrational submission and denigration of self, Satan separates himself from God and thereby damns himself since the blind fury of his pride causes him to revolt without having heeded the meaning of the Son's exaltation. He reacts to the Son's elevation by trying to elevate himself. Knowing full well that he cannot revolt against God's omnipotence, he seizes on the Son's elevation, for he wants the happiness of being raised closer to God but chooses not to see that such happiness is available to him through the Messiah. In contrast to most theologians, Milton held that evil came into being when Lucifer envied the Son without knowing about man and the Redemption. Satan is aware of the Son as heavenly king, not as human savior, and he envies God's goodness to man only after he has lost Heaven. If Satan is envious not of the Incarnation but of the Son, why has the Son prompted Satan's dual reaction of envy and hate? In one sense, the question is unanswerable. If God has provoked Satan's jealousy, this sin's cause has to be jealousy itself. Jealousy, like Sin in Book 2, is "a monster / Begot upon itself, born of itself" (*Othello*, 3.4.161–62). According to Revard, Milton suggests an additional explanation, implying that the Son's kingly role signifies divine love and grace, but Satan sees this kingship not as love but as an enviable office that he wants for himself. He resents the Son's person and desires his kingly office. Though Milton makes it clear that the Son's power comes from his person, not his office as Son, Satan rejects the Son's person and hence divine love. By refusing to know who the Son really is, he creates his own kingdom of darkness.[34] From this impending darkness, Abdiel at the end of the book departs.

## Book 6

For many readers the war in Heaven is a poetic problem: Did Milton need to treat the battle of warring spirits in such extensive physical detail? The episode occupies nearly a tenth of the total length of the poem—far more than its importance might seem to warrant. Yet Milton's Christian theme required that the Son be seen in triumph over the rebel angels; this victory over evil occurs at the exact center of the epic. Raphael's detailed account of the war is needed as a warning to Adam and Eve about obedience; it is also a structural and thematic climax that provides a foreshadowing of the Second Coming of Christ at the end of time, a positive indication that goodness will indeed come out of evil. Because the creation of man, as well as his temptation, fall, and redemption, results from Satan's rebellion and fall, the war in Heaven makes Book 6 the cornerstone of the epic.

For all the book's serious, thematic importance, however, comic ridicule is a basic element in Milton's Heaven. Satan's being wounded and thereby ridiculed by Michael, paralleling his ridicule by Gabriel in Book 4, is a psychological debasement comparable to the animal forms he is forced to assume. Milton, a master of incongruity, also helps the reader see the absurdity of Satan's assertion of physical force against the Almighty. Evil comes from disobedience and results in violence and war. Hence the efforts of Satan to invent and use gunpowder are an especially ludicrous climax to his revolt against God's unshakable throne.

Readers who, like Samuel Johnson, have found the war to be poetic nonsense underestimate both Milton's sense of ironic ridicule and his use of metaphor. The poet's disapproval of epic military valor does not prevent its use to heighten the absurdity of a futile war, which repeatedly shows the justice of God and the freedom of creatures to choose to rebel. If taken literally, the cannons, chariots, weapons, and angelic wounds are laughable, yet the poet uses anthropomorphic, accommodated concepts and terms to show these "invisible exploits," which are beyond the comprehension of even unfallen man. The angels' ability to assume corporeal forms does not lead to the loss of their spiritual essence when a third of them search for and use (metaphorically) physical means to wage their moral-spiritual battle. That pure spirits become "gross by sinning," weighed down by materiality, is both intentionally absurd and incongruous and a continuation of Milton's hierarchy of spirit, seen in Book 5, whereby matter is constantly being perfected. In this way Milton, by comparing "spiritual to corporal forms," produces a metaphoric means of relating to Adam and Eve (and the reader) "what surmounts the reach / Of human sense" (5.571–73). Like Adam, we listen in wonder to "things so high and strange. . . . So unimaginable as hate in Heav'n" (7.53–54).

As Raphael describes how Abdiel hastens from the rebels' camp with news of Satan's insurrection, he explains Heaven's alternating light and dark, resembling day and night on Earth, so that the morning is described as golden when Abdiel finds the gleaming angelic squadrons already prepared for war. He is welcomed by the good angels as the faithful servant whose courage in standing up to Satan causes rejoicing in Heaven. Milton uses various scriptural sources in having God command the loyalty of Abdiel, who, in fighting the good fight (2 Timothy 4.7), has defended truth, which is mightier than the sword. He must now perform the "easier" task of defeating those who had scorned his virtuous stance in divorcing himself from Satan's rebellion. Divine justice limits the power of the defense: Michael and Gabriel are to lead the "invincible" angels, equal in number to the rebellious forces. The heavenly powers move in disciplined unity to the sound of instrumental harmony. The image of birds "in orderly array" signals that Adam is listening to Raphael's narrative in Eden, whose harmony reflects Heaven's, and that, while Satan is preparing to strike Adam and Eve, the reader hears about the adversary's earlier, parallel attack and imminent fall.

In contrast to the orderly march of the loyal angels, the rebels move with furious speed, foolishly thinking that they can defeat God in a surprise attack. In their midst sits Satan "exalted" as a rival deity in a gaudy parody of the Messiah's chariot of divine power. Abdiel is outraged that Satan, still resplendent in heavenly gold and diamonds despite his disloyalty, is idolized by his followers, who should be worshiping the true image of God in the Son. The faithful angel tells himself that he must wage a violent battle with Satan since the apostate's reason has been found false. He then defies him in a speech typical of epic warriors before battle, calling Satan a fool for vainly daring to fight God. In speaking of his own loyalty to God, Abdiel reflects Milton's personal conviction that a minority of one carries strength. Satan returns the mockery with scorn, ironically calling Abdiel a "seditious Angel" who opposed a synod of heavenly "Gods." He who is to be enslaved sees the obedience of the good angels as servitude and his own rebellious forces as free since he contends that those who serve God are lazy. Abdiel sternly responds, noting Satan's confusion of obedience with servitude as well as his impudence in mocking heavenly worship, then strikes the first blow, which is too swift, Raphael explains, to be seen. The weakness of Satan shocks his troops; he recoils in a movement that can only be compared to a mountain of pines being overturned. Milton, wishing to make his heavenly battle comprehensible, is forced to describe the fury and clamor in the martial style of the classical epics that he intends to surpass; yet the folly of Satan is consistently highlighted by the irony of this futile war. Of course, Heaven and Earth shake, Raphael explains; what else would happen when millions of fierce angels fight? God, controlling the events, limits their power so that Heaven will not be ravaged. In excited style, Raphael describes the warfare in which "deeds of eternal fame" are performed by mighty warriors on the ground and in the air, evenly matched until Satan encounters Michael. The princely spirit calls Satan the "Author of evil" who, unknown until he rebelled, is ordered to Hell for corrupting thousands. Responding to these "airy threats," Satan contends that he will wage a successful battle since his forces are undefeated.

As they prepare to resume the fight, Milton through Raphael again calls attention to the inadequacy of human language in describing an indescribable contest. The analogy of conflicting planets causing cosmic discord suggests the magnitude of this immense battle. The reader, wondering how such violent discord could exist in Heaven, needs to be reminded that, although Milton's war also involves the good angels in the ridicule of physical battle, the action must be taken metaphorically.

Michael's mighty sword wounds the archrebel. Satan's first humiliating experience of pain causes him shame; but the wound of an angelic being, Raphael explains, quickly heals since the invulnerable spirits can perish only by annihilation, even if they choose corporeal faculties. Meanwhile Gabriel and the other good angels fight the rebels, some of whom bear the names of heathen gods (as in 1.374–521), the others being condemned to eternal silence. As the first phase of the battle ends, the rebels have been wounded and weakened, whereas the loyalists, invincible because of their virtue, are not susceptible to fatigue or pain.

As both sides retire, Satan, restless, calls a night meeting to reassure his companions that, having been tested on the first day of battle, they cannot be defeated. Not content with liberty, he says, they seek glory and dominion. Unaware of the disastrous rout they suffered and of the divinely limited forces they have encountered, he is convinced that they are imperishable since his own wound has quickly healed. The next speaker is called Nisroch, after an Assyrian vulture god. Nisroch tells the assembled rebels that their "matchless" strength is worthless when one is weakened by pain and that some invention is needed to injure the enemy since the fight so far has been uneven. If his cohorts are concerned about pain, Satan says that the minerals under the ground of Heaven will produce the "implements of mischief" needed to crush the foe. That Satan is to invent gunpowder and the rebels to use artillery adds to the irony. "The absurd physical violence of Milton's devils and angels becomes all the more striking in contrast with the symbolic power of truth that is represented in their overthrow by the Son of God."[35]

As the devils secretly begin to dig for minerals, Raphael warns Adam of "dev'lish machination" on Earth, reminding us of the parallel between the heavenly fable and the human situation. Milton and his contemporaries thought of angels as armed and winged male warriors; thus the description of helmets, shields, and breastplates would be familiar. In contrast to the loyalists' light, orderly march, the rebels move "with heavy pace," dragging along their hidden artillery. Equally devious is Satan's claim that the rebels seek a peaceful settlement. Then, with the cannon belching forth a thunderous blast, hail and thunderbolts topple the loyalists, who disperse. Boastful Satan mocks his foes for running away, and Belial briefly joins in the scoffing. Anger prompts the faithful hosts to fly to the hills where they uproot rocks and trees, hurling them onto their foes' cannon, destroying the source of their confidence. God, whose permissive will has already determined what has occurred, remains secure, knowing that the anointed Son's mission will be fulfilled. The heroic role of Messiah as the expression of the Father's love and mercy begins and expands as the poem unfolds. With the Father necessarily distant, the Son becomes the instrument for bridging the gap between God and man, for whom the heavenly war is both a lesson in obedience and a prefiguring of Christ's redemptive action.

The centrality of Christ as the highest embodiment of Milton's heroic ideal is revealed in the Son's heavenly victory at the climax of Raphael's long lesson to Adam at the center of the epic. His triumph over the rebel angels expresses his divine exaltation, fulfilling the promise of Book 3.305–322. The Messiah's dramatic action, for which he has waited in patient obedience, suggests that the earthly heroism of the Redeemer can be applied to the Son in eternity. Raphael's education of Adam is to be completed by Michael in Books 11 and 12, bringing into focus the poem's theme of the redemptive power of love and obedience. Thus the two angelic lessons are linked for Adam and the reader.

The Father, speaking to the Son as the expression of his inexpressible glory, explains that the war has been allowed to proceed this far so that the Son would have the glory of ending it, demonstrating his power as anointed king. Divine interference is necessary to prevent ongoing disorder, and the Son has been given matchless power. In a passage rich in biblical allusions, the Messiah appears on the third day of the battle as majestic judge. He is also the victorious savior, whose resurrection on the third day will signify his triumph over sin and death. The Son's climactic heavenly victory not only inverts the false heroism of Satan and his followers but also anticipates the triumph of the Messiah as earthly redeemer and as judge. Biblical prophecy (Zechariah 12.10 and Revelation 1.7) links the crucified Christ with the Christ of the Second Coming, both prefigured in his heavenly victory. The Messiah is seated in a four-wheeled throne-chariot decorated with animals described in Ezekiel (1.5–13), signifying the harmony brought by the Son to the four corners of the world. In contrast to the tumult, smoke, and disorder caused by the fallen angels, the Son rides to triumph as the light of the world. But the rebels, envious of his glory, remain perversely obstinate.

Speaking to the faithful forces, the Son asserts that he alone can punish the rebels, whose scorn, envy, and rage have been directed at his exaltation by the Father. Then, bearing God's wrath, he looses "ten thousand Thunders," depriving the evil angels of all resistance and courage. "Exhausted, spiritless, afflicted, fallen," they drop their weapons in defeat. But the Son limits his force since his aim is to drive them out of Heaven, not to destroy them. Like goats they are herded together before throwing themselves through an opening in Heaven's wall. The poetic climax of the action (867–77) is a vivid description of the fall of the rebel angels, the conclusion of the Son's victory. He then rides in triumph amid the loyal angels bearing palm branches, as he will later ride into Jerusalem.

Raphael ends his story with a reminder that it cannot be taken literally but as a warning since Satan is also plotting how to seduce man from faithful obedience. Thus the lesson for Adam is clear: be firm in avoiding overly high aspirations, temptations, and disobedience.

## Book 7

The second half of the epic opens with another of Milton's invocations, signaling both a transition in Raphael's narrative and a reminder of the poet's personal concern with creating a Christian poem that transcends the limits of the classical imagination. He again calls upon heavenly wisdom, symbolized by Urania, by whose aid he has soared to Heaven, a daring feat that seems to have taxed his strength. If he is to return to earth to sing the second part of his song, he will need supernatural aid so that he can persist in his task and not fall, dazed and blind, like Bellerophon, who tried to explore the mysteries of the heavens on winged Pegasus. Milton's fear of his own possible fall, heightened by the "evil days" of post-Restoration disillusionment, points up an interesting parallel between the poet's soaring flight, proclaimed in the initial invocation, and the ascent and descent of both Satan and Adam. Throughout the poem, physical and spiritual wandering, aspiration, and fall are recurring motifs. The poet's song has been a journey into "Things unattempted yet," into both light and darkness, heightened by his physical blindness, as he attempts to forge a new vocabulary for expressing the inexpressible. He has been careful to distinguish his own aspiration from Satan's proud blindness and dark descent while depicting the wandering thoughts of Adam and Eve that lead to exile from ideal happiness. Thus this third invocation reminds us of several simultaneous levels of drama in the poem: the tragic plot of Satan, the tragicomic plot of Adam, whose Fall leads to reconciliation, and the heavenly drama of the Son. More obvious is the drama of Milton wrestling with his own emotional darkness and loneliness; against such a background, one wonders how the poetic persona can complete his ambitious poem. The poet shaping and controlling the action is present to an unusually extensive degree in his epic.

The reader is given a brief recapitulation of the war in Heaven and its lesson, which is a positive injunction to love and not to fear. Raphael's gentle emphasis in the war narrative has been less on rebellion than on obedience through love, as seen in the extensive role of Abdiel. The reader is now told that Adam has listened, astonished and reflective, to Raphael's narrative. Grateful to have discovered what unaided "human knowledge could not reach" and aware of the need for obedience, Adam retains innocent curiosity that, as Raphael points out, must be governed by temperance: Adam must ask about "knowledge within bounds." In inquiring why God "so late" created the world, the tentative Adam must still learn how to ask about proper knowledge, not the abstruse secrets of God. The warning about temperate inquiry (126–30) is important both for Adam's continuing education and for the poem's lesson about vain aspiration.

The seraph, revealing what will help man know and serve God, begins his story with the Father surveying the results of Satan's failed rebellion and telling the Son that not only are there abundant good angels to fill Heaven but that he will create another world and another race of creatures who will be tested in obedience and given the chance to return to Heaven. (This chance, however, will be lost because of the Fall.) Creation is to be performed by the Son as the Word of God. The Father also proclaims that the world will emerge from Chaos, from which God, though unlimited, will withdraw his influence since his goodness is free to act or not to act. Creation can therefore be metaphorically represented as "a divine excursion into a region of apparent otherness" where his goodness is not operative.[36]

As in most biblical commentary, the creation is instantaneous but revealed in stages, in the six days of creation from Genesis, which the poet paraphrases and amplifies. Heaven rejoices at the news with words that echo the angels' "Glory to God in the highest" at Christ's birth (Luke 2.14). The emphasis on the Son as "Word" (175.208, etc.) also indicates a parallel between the Creation and the Incarnation ("In the beginning was the word. . . . And the Word was made flesh," John 1.1, 14). The radiant majesty of the Son in Heaven, reflecting the Father's wisdom and love, is seen as he rides forth into Chaos. Milton has used Psalm 24 to depict the King of Glory; he now adds to the Genesis account of creation the image (from Proverbs 8) of God as architect of the universe, drawing a compass or circle on the face of the deep. The Son's voice and hand mark the universal boundaries, but the Spirit of God, with the "brooding wings" cited in the opening invocation (1.20–21), impregnates unformed matter. The dove that will descend on Christ at his baptism and that now moves the formless matter at the world's creation is the "same

Spirit invoked by the poet to give shape and substance to the formless matter in the mind, of which the poem is to be made."[37]

God speaks the word and thereby creates light, which is then separated from darkness. On the second day the firmament is created. For Milton this was the mass of air and vapor between the earth and the outermost vault of the created universe. On the third day, Earth is compared to a fetus surrounded in the womb by water, which, being active, shapes the globe with life-giving fluid. Fertilized by the sea, Earth is metaphorically born when God says, "Let dry land appear"; mountains emerge, and the waters fill the valleys with a rush like that of marching armies. Still following the Genesis account, Milton describes the creation of plants and trees with some of the same rich language used to describe man (4.304–8) since Earth now seems a Heaven where "Gods might dwell."

On the fourth day (Genesis 1.14–19) lights are created in the firmament to regulate the temporal division between day and night. The sun drinks in much of the liquid light already created and becomes a "Palace" of light from which the stars acquire their own radiance. In describing the dawn and stars dancing before the cheerful sun, Milton again embellishes the biblical creation story while remaining faithful to its spirit. Moving up the scale of being, he next depicts the genesis of animal life. The poet adds colorful details to his catalogue to suggest the plentitude of nature's goodness.

Milton, who perhaps saw paintings of animals emerging "full grown" from the earth, retains the image of the Earth's womb from which are born innumerable living creatures. Given special emphasis is the wily serpent, but like all animals, Raphael says, it is obedient to Adam, a point forgotten in the temptation. The Earth smiles at the complete beauty of creation, but the "Master work," man—not "prone" but upright and superior because of the "Sanctity of Reason"—remains to be created. Man is made in God's image from the "Dust of the ground"; the very substance of his being is related to the world of which he is a part. Created outside the garden, he is brought into it and given dominion over the Earth. Adam's lordship over creation, his superiority to the animals, is important because of the serpent's upcoming claims. We then hear the unambiguous edict against partaking of the fruit of the tree that brings knowledge of good and evil.

God's return to Heaven after completing the creation is heralded by celestial music and an angelic chorus of praise that links Heaven and Earth in harmonious accord. The process of creation is thus intended to be an upward development from earthly garden to heavenly paradise, bringing new goodness out of the evil caused by the rebel angels. The angels sing of "Thrice happy men," who are made in God's likeness to dwell and worship him, to rule and multiply, and to know of their own idyllic happiness. The vast universe contains numberless stars, each a potential world; hearing this gives Adam the clue to ask about other planets. But Raphael has answered his request for the story of creation, which we are invited to admire for its beauty and bounty in a poem full of praise and gratitude.

## Book 8

As if awakening from the spell of Raphael's words, Adam thanks the angelic visitor for satisfying his great thirst for knowledge, but he is still filled with wonder and doubt about the vastness of space in comparison with the relative insignificance of the tiny Earth that seems to remain still while greater planets daily encircle it. He is astonished by the apparent disproportion in the universe, implying that Nature (and God) have somehow erred. Adam's questions and Raphael's answers reflect Milton's own lifelong interest in astronomy. While relying for poetic purposes on the traditional Ptolemaic, geocentric cosmology, the poet nevertheless includes many references in the epic to the then new scientific discoveries of Galileo, Copernicus, Kepler, and others. That the poet's imagination was stirred by such discoveries is apparent from his fascination with the telescope and with vast spatial perspectives, yet he maintained a more conservative sense of a measurable, circumscribed world in which God, not space, is infinite. The rich interplay between old and new conceptions of space in Milton's work presents a dual perspective whereby Earth as viewed by man is contrasted with its perception from afar. As Nicolson observes, for later poets the sublime achievement of Milton was not his concept of God and Satan, Heaven and Hell but his sense of space and "the vast reaches of the cosmic imagination."[38]

Adam has "studious thoughts abstruse," which for Milton can lead to vain curiosity rather than proper knowledge. Eve is intellectually capable of, and interested in, such discourse but she prefers to hear it from her husband, who would make the presentation more personal and pleasurable. Her departure here, like that in Book 9 (385–98), is suggestively regal and "Goddess-like," the poet implying both her innocence and allure, her potentially dangerous charms as well as her charming graces.

The angel then tells Adam that many of God's secrets demand wonder rather than investigation. Since all creation serves man's needs, the brighter sun is not necessarily superior; it serves man by producing fruitful life on Earth. The vastness of space and the speed of the heavenly bodies testify to God's power. That the planets move around the still Earth affirms man's perspective, Raphael says, which cannot embrace the divine mystery of creation; man must not presume to overreach his limited faculties. The angelic teacher is more concerned with Adam's attitude of inquiry than with providing final answers to his questions.

Raphael now presents the heliocentric, Copernican view to counter Adam's doubts about the Ptolemaic universe and his objection to a vast system of planets whose only apparent function is to shed light on Earth. But in treating the new scientific theory as only a hypothesis, Raphael emphasizes what is relevant to the coming temptation to higher knowledge. The lesson is clear (159–78): whether or not the Earth moves or the sun rises is irrelevant to a happy life; such speculations touch on hidden knowledge proper only to God, not man, who must not "reach too high" but be "lowly wise." Milton, while not opposing scientific curiosity, is more concerned with ethics than astronomy; natural human speculation, he believes, requires temperate guidance so that knowledge will promote living virtuously. Adam now feels free of "all anxious cares" since he has learned to avoid "perplexing thoughts."

Having grasped the lesson about proper knowledge, Adam proposes to tell his own story. He seems eager to detain the seraph, who is interested in and impressed by human nature. (This compliment to man is to be perverted by Satan's envy.) Adam clearly enjoys displaying the fruits of reason in his own words to a superior guest. In having Raphael address Adam as a "fellow servant" honored by God, Milton alludes to the angel's words to John in

Revelation 22.8–9. Since he was absent when man was created, having been sent to "fast shut" the gates of Hell, Raphael is delighted to hear Adam's story.

In a beautiful amplification of the spare Genesis account, Milton has Adam describe his first sense of self-awareness and of the beauties of the newly created Earth. His reaction to his life is one of joy followed by humility when he realizes that he is indebted to "some great Maker." In a dream paralleling Eve's dream in Book 5, he is led by a "shape Divine" to the blissful garden, more beautiful than the area he saw before he slept, whereupon he wakes to discover that reality has replaced the dream. As in the Bible (Genesis 2.15–17), God reveals himself to Adam and gives him paradise with the sole command not to eat of the Tree of Knowledge, set as a test of obedience close by the Tree of Life. Given lordship over creation, he is able with infused knowledge to name the animals. But his pleasure is limited since he is alone. God then enjoys testing him in a playful question-and-answer exchange. Adam expresses dissatisfaction with the company of animals, who have mates while he lacks fellowship. Whereas man is limited by being single, God, Adam recognizes, has no such deficiency. Dependence on God is a source of strength for man, yet man's dependence on his fellow creatures is a source of potential weakness, as is seen in Adam's upcoming fear of losing Eve; as a result, he will listen to her rather than to his reason.

God is pleased with Adam's forthright speech, admitting that He has been testing him, a significant prologue to the coming test of obedience; Adam has shown himself aware of his superiority to the animals and capable of withstanding God's gentle temptation. Exhausted from this exchange, Adam is allowed to sleep with his imagination waking so that, in a trance, he can witness the birth of Eve from his left side, a positive counterpart to Sin emerging from the left side of Satan (2.755). Like the Son, she bears the image of the one from whom she proceeds and represents reconciling love.

Adam excitedly recalls the "love and amorous delight" he finds in Eve's beauty, preferring her to "other pleasures." A man deeply in love, he thanks God for this fairest of gifts, then pursues her to the nuptial bower. Nature rejoices at this new union, which reflects divine love. In trying to describe to the angel his new sensation of rapture and "passion," he reveals the potential danger of his weakness in the face of the "charm of Beauty's powerful glance." Though recognizing the woman's natural inferiority, he is "Transported" by her physical appeals, fearful that her beauty may lead him astray, for such loveliness is unequaled in creation. He is aware that Eve's beauty challenges his rational self-control, and Raphael reminds him not to disrespect the hierarchy of love by placing Eve before himself and God nor to overvalue sexual pleasure. The woman's physical beauty is meant as a source of love and honor; the man must not be so in awe of her as to have his judgment weaken in her presence.

Adam is still learning as his dialogue with Raphael draws to a close. "Half-abasht," he tries to explain that his complex feelings for Eve are more than sexual. Then, since the angel has described earthly love as leading to heavenly love, Adam asks about angelic love. In what has seemed to many readers a poetically imprudent or unnecessary episode, Raphael blushes with the rosy glow of love. He has encouraged Adam's seemingly presumptuous question and responds in terms consistent with the poem's metaphorical conception of pure spirits: angels enjoy every happiness man does, including the possibility of embracing and mixing their aerial "bodies."

Raphael concludes the long education of Adam, begun in Book 5, with a warning to be strong, lest passion overcome reason. Man's ability "to stand or fall" lies in the power of his free will.

## Book 9

The final invocation (1–47) sets the stage for the epic's most dramatic book and signals a transition from the education of Adam in Books 5–8 to the climactic temptation. In contrast to the pleasant, "familiar" exchange between angel and man, the poet emphasizes the "distance" to come between Heaven and Earth as the result of sin. His rich wordplay (*distrust, disloyal, disobedience*) ends with *distaste,* recalling the sin announced at the beginning of Book 1: man's taste of the forbidden fruit will lead to God's distaste for, and alienation from, man.

Calling upon the divine wisdom of his "celestial Patroness" for the last time, Milton asks for an appropriate style for his "Sad task," a task greater ("more Heroic") than the siege of Troy told in the *Iliad* or the wanderings of Aeneas or of Odysseus. The challenge to earlier epics leads to the most explicit definition of Milton's notion of Christian heroism. After some delay because of a reluctance to describe military valor, he says that he has chosen what others have neglected to celebrate: the more important subject of spiritual strength ("Patience and Heroic Martyrdom"). Aided by the Spirit who visits him as he sleeps, the poet hopes that his "higher Argument" will find the renown he seeks, trusting that it is not too late for him and for his age to hear great heroic poetry.

Satan's return to Eden under the cloak of darkness continues the narrative from the end of Book 4, where Satan had fled from a useless showdown with Gabriel. While the reader was hearing from Raphael of the war in Heaven and the Creation, Satan was strengthening his "malice and fraud," ready to seek "Man's destruction." After seven nights of circling the Earth, he found "by stealth" an unseen entrance: After hiding in one of the underground rivers, then being wrapped in a mist, he has carefully chosen the "wily Snake" as the least suspect creature. His ironic apostrophe to the Earth again links Book 9 with Book 4, where Satan had addressed the sun and revealed his own contrasting despair. After the long interval of Books 5–8, his present speech of lament and envy is thus a necessary reminder of the satanic mind. He has changed little; in fact, his rhetoric, used before, now seems stale. This speech soon turns typically to the self as Satan realizes again how painful his torment is in contrast with the "Pleasure" he views. Boasting that he will "in one day" ruin what God had created in six, he imagines his inflated glory in Hell. He then claims that he freed from bondage nearly half of the angelic host. Satan, who once felt some guilt for his actions, lies to himself, confusing enslavement with freedom. He is so consumed with hatred for God and envy of man's creation that (at 146–47) he wonders if God created the angels, who now guard man's magnificent world. As he is about to descend into the serpent, Satan curses his own ambitious revenge that requires him to undergo such debasement. Milton's use of *incarnate* (166) has ironic implication for the reader, who knows that the Son's Incarnation will redeem the effects of Satan's "foul descent."

Since the temptation will be spoken, it is apt that Satan enters the sleeping serpent "in at his Mouth"; thus concealed, he waits, his final metamorphosis complete. As soon as dawn comes, Eve tells Adam that the work of tending the garden, which, she says, has become "luxurious," "overgrown," "wanton," and almost "wild," is too much for them. She proposes that they separate since, she claims, being together provides distractions. This idea seems to reflect Eve's desire to win control of her husband, to be his intellectual equal now that Raphael is gone. The separation reflects the potential for disorder in Eden, for it upsets the temporal order of their daily lives, reverses the traditional male-female hierarchy, and anticipates the Fall itself.

Eve errs in trying to improve on nature rather than obeying the law of God as upheld by Adam. She presents a skillful argument but is wrong in putting work first. For Milton every action should lead one to God, not to the self. Adam's husbandly function, which she rejects, is to help Eve grow toward God through him. Thus he tries to explain that work is not an end in itself and that God would provide more aid if the garden really needs the attention that seems to concern her. It is their love, not their labor, that will lead them to increase their knowledge of God. But he does not follow his own advice and so fails as the rational guide and protector, assuming some of Eve's impatience just as she tries to move higher on the chain of being. Overly zealous, Eve assumes the male role when Adam is unable to cope with her arguments, which require a control he lacks. Allegorically, Adam represents Eve's reason and she his love; their separation will weaken their symbiotic union.

Adam's first, long response (227–69) indicates doubts and fears as he tells Eve that their distracting "looks and smiles" are natural and good since God made them to delight, not toil, in their work. Moreover, he reminds her that a foe envying their happiness might harm her if they work apart. After hearing Adam urge her not to leave his side, Eve remains firm, a queenly figure with "sweet austere composure," as if she expected Adam's automatic approval of her plan. She says she did not expect to hear Adam doubt her "firmness" merely because of a foe they were warned about. Why, she asks, fear violence since we are incapable of death and pain? She believes that Adam fears their enemy's deceptiveness and distrusts her love and faith; by presuming that she cannot fall, she reveals weakness. Affected by the growth of the garden, Eve has used logic in advocating separation for the sake of her relationship with Adam. Now, however, in an important change, she abandons reason in favor of the passions, as the emotional, personal nature of her words (at 279–81) reveal, prompting an emotional response from Adam. The ideal balance between reason and emotion will be more fully upset when Adam and Eve experience a conflict between what they know to be wrong and what they vainly desire: to satisfy their own feelings and curiosity. The entire discussion of security has heightened irony and tension for the reader, who is aware of Satan's presence, the result of his ability to penetrate the "secure" garden.

Adam's epithets for his wife, like hers for him, are elaborate, a sign of weakened security. Addressing her as "immortal Eve" (291), the last time he can do so, Adam asserts the joint strength of their marital union. But, still feeling that he undervalues her faith and security, Eve declares that an enemy would hurt only himself, not them, and that they cannot have their happiness limited by some potential evil. Feeling overly confident, she reflects the false sense of security on which Satan can work, for she concludes that, contrary to the lesson provided by Raphael, God would not leave them unable to stand alone. A temptation would be an insult, she says; virtue untested is worthless. A central point in this discussion of security is that man should not be too secure (literally, *without care*), too independent or self-sufficient, since obedience implies dependence on God. As Adam's response indicates, the real threat is not external but "within."

In reminding her of their free will and the need to be watchful ("erect"), Adam tries to use reason and the theoretical knowledge he has to counter her persuasive arguments. But what he says is not forceful enough, lecturing rather than asserting his role as husband. Reason tells him that they should work together to avoid the "trial," but frustrated by her stubbornness, he gives in. As line 1156 makes clear, Adam does not command Eve "absolutely not to go"; such a lawful command would give her the freedom to obey or disobey. Instead of forbidding her to leave, he orders her to leave. This important exchange reflects the complexities of human decision making: if Eve had known more, she would have been as suspicious as her better-informed husband says they should be, yet she could not have known more without eating of the tree of knowledge.

Persistent Eve has the last word. Noting Adam's weak concession that a test "when least sought" might find them "far less prepared," she is even more confident of her conviction that to work independently will not invite temptation. Firm but gentle, she withdraws her hand, severing herself from her "Author and Disposer" (4.635). Preferring independence to obedience, she is vulnerable to the inevitable temptation. As Eve departs she is compared to several pagan, mythological goddesses, suggesting the fallen world. Though promising to return by noon, she will upset the ordered cycle of their life and her innocence, the poet says in his lament (404–11) for "hapless Eve."

Satan in the form of the serpent discovers Eve alone but is too struck by her beauty to consider his good fortune. She stands in a "Cloud of Fragrance," supporting the fair, fragile flowers, symbolizing mutability. The weakness she tries to remedy in the flowers is revealingly transferred to Eve, pictured as physically and morally frail.

The serpent draws nearer, moving sinuously toward Eve in the garden, seen as "more delicious" than other paradises. As Satan recognizes, it reflects Heaven, as does Eve, an inseparable part of the garden. The tempter, struck by the beauty of paradise, is more awed by the woman's beauty. Much like a city dweller enjoying a sudden breath of country air, he is briefly removed from his evil pollution. The experience of goodness soon reminds him of the Hell within, and he is tormented by what he cannot have. In his soliloquy (473–93) Satan must remind himself that he came not for admiration but for destruction; he is glad the man is absent, Satan hating to admit that Adam is stronger than he (486–87). In calling her "divinely fair, fit Love for Gods," Satan develops the seductive appeal of his temptation.

Milton would have been aware of artistic and theological treatments of the serpent's upright posture, the sexual overtones reinforced by the myths the poet cites of gods "chang'd" (transformed) into serpents. Milton's masterful use of enjambment (494–526) gives these lines a sinuous appearance and sound, paralleling both the movement of the serpent and Satan's guileful argument in his upcoming temptation. As the serpent moves slowly toward Eve, she is charmed by his beauty; his "circling spires" or coils float across the grass in a display of sensual loveliness. Milton was aware of a Jewish tradition by which Eve had sex with the Serpent and so makes him erotically appealing. The poet, again likening Satan to a seafarer (513) or wanderer looking for solace from his misery, also uses a navigational image as the devil tries to steer his way into Eve's heart. The veering ship simile adds to the sense of movement as Satan virtually dances before Eve to "lure her Eye." Bowing his crested head, he flatters her by licking the ground; Satan would not bow down before the Son in Heaven but now ironically debases himself by fawning over an earthly creature.

Satan falsely addresses Eve as "sole wonder" and "Sovereign mistress" (in fact, Adam has been given dominion over Eden); equally false is his claim that she is "universally admired" as a "Goddess among gods." Having listened to Adam and Eve in their supposedly secure paradise, Satan picks up Adam's words in line 539, praising Eve's beauty. She should be able to see through his words, but, unaccustomed to flattery, she is overwhelmed by his speech. His words work on her subconscious as foreshadowed in her dream (in Book 5). She is so amazed by the serpent's speech that she fails to listen to what he says. As in her dream, Eve's vanity is vulnerable: he calls her "resplendent" but also uses the temptations to power ("Empress") and to knowledge ("to tell thee all").

Satan's description of the fruit and its power is filled with sensual excitement as he tells Eve that the fruit of the forbidden tree gave him human speech. He claims to have aspired higher than his place, implying that she too can aspire and that she will enjoy, as he has, "such pleasure." The appeal to go beyond the restraints of temperance to satisfy her physical desire is coupled with an intellectual appeal to transcend the limits of human nature. That the fruit is high on the tree, requiring a reach upward beyond licit bounds, is an important symbolic feature captured in many paintings of this scene. (See figure 3, p. 138.)

He concludes his second speech of temptation by again appealing to Eve's vanity, calling her the fairest of creatures, a queen to be worshiped. Admitting that the serpent's lavish praise causes her to question his claims, she is curious to see this amazing tree. Pleased to be called "Empress," she tells the serpent to "Lead then," having rejected Adam's leadership; she further upsets the natural hierarchy by following an animal. Eve develops with the serpent-tempter the relationship she should have maintained with her husband.

The serpent revealingly makes the path to sin easy (he "made the intricate seem straight"). Glowing, the tempter resembles the evil spirits associated in folklore with the light, produced by marsh gas, that leads simple people astray. Seeing the tree, Eve observes that the visit is "Fruitless" since the tree is forbidden and that the only proof ("credit") of the fruit's power is what the serpent has said. She is aware of the ironic significance of "excess" (intemperance) and of the play on the word *fruit,* which also means *result;* she is also oblivious to Satan's repeatedly perverse use of the word *fair.* As Hughes notes, her use of the Hebrew expression "Sole Daughter of his voice" (654) for God's command shows that she is softening the prohibition, seeing it as having less weight than an absolute command.[39] And she wrongly claims that she and Adam are a law unto themselves: reason is not their only law.

Satan, seizing upon her certainty and vulnerability, at once suggests that the command is unreasonable, and her brief response merely repeats God's words, without conviction. As if moved by concern for man and outrage at such an unjust law, Satan, like some eloquent orator, raises himself up. By venturing higher than his place, he says, he is not punished for having touched and tasted the forbidden tree. He minimizes the penalty for such a "petty Trespass" as well as the existence of the death he has fathered. He questions the reality of evil and the possibility of not knowing evil except by experience. Claiming next that God is just and so cannot punish without cause, he at the same time says that God is not just if He punishes; thus He is not to be obeyed. Moving too swiftly to give Eve a chance to think, he then claims that such an unreasonable edict was meant to keep her "low and ignorant." At the heart of his overwhelming argument is that even God knows that

> Your Eyes that seem so clear,
> Yet are but dim shall perfectly be then
> Op'n'd and clear'd, and ye shall be as Gods,
> Knowing both good and evil as they know. (706–9)

Compare at this point the biblical text [Genesis 3.4–7] in the King James version used by Milton:

> And the serpent said unto the woman, Ye shall not surely die: For God doth know that in the day ye eat thereof, then your eyes shall be opened, and ye shall be as gods, knowing good and evil. And when the woman saw that the tree was good for food, and that it was pleasant to the eyes, and a tree to be desired to make one wise, she took of the fruit thereof, and did eat. And the eyes of them both were opened, and they knew that they were naked.

Satan, pretending that death will mean an ascent to the divine, appeals to vision as a source of wisdom, but the reverse will occur: Adam and Eve's spiritual vision declines following the sin. Satan concludes his long speech by again suggesting the foolishness of God's law as well as Eve's "need" of this "fair" fruit. Sin is called Satan's "fair daughter" (in 10.352), pointing up the irony and ambivalence of this satanically perverted word.

The poet says that the serpent's guileful words find a "too easy" entrance into Eve's heart as she looks at the fruit and hears these seemingly "persuasive words." Her vulnerability to such language is heightened by her hunger, having missed her noon meal. In her address to the tree (745–79), the effects of her earlier dream and the tempter's words overcome her reason. She believes Satan's idea that the tree has been "too long" forbidden, and since God unreasonably forbids one to know and "be wise," she concludes, His command is not binding. Eve dismisses the death penalty since the serpent has eaten and not only lives but, she thinks, has achieved the higher level of being that she desires for herself. Ironically, she calls the serpent "Author unsuspect" (771), but Adam is her true source or "Author" (4.653) just as God is the "Author of this Universe" (8.360). Her mind tainted, she blindly imagines God as the envious source of death, unaware that the serpent is the "Author of evil" (6.262) to whom she is now subject.

It is not a mere poetic device that Nature feels the "wound" of Eve's sin: Disobedience will lead to fallen Nature. Totally absorbed in her newfound pleasure, which is heightened by great expectations, Eve "greedily" eats, thinking that the fruit will be miraculous. In fact, she eats death as she adds the sin of concupiscence (lawless appetite) to pride and disobedience. In her speech to the tree (795–810), Eve, who was once in harmony with Nature, now worships it. Confused, she uses Satan's equivocal word *Gods,* thinking she has found maturity and wisdom. Her view of God as a "great forbidder" is as tainted as her logic, and she wonders if she should keep this secret of "Full happiness" to herself and be superior ("more equal") to Adam. Selfishly concluding that he would likely get another wife, she decides to share her discovery with Adam.

He meanwhile has been weaving a garland of "choicest Flow'rs" as if to crown Eve, whose absence troubles his heart (845). She too has a bough in her hand from the forbidden tree; there he finds her flushed and agitated, as her breathless speech (856–85) indicates. Aware of her guilt for missing their noon meal, she claims to have missed him, too, but is late for a "wonderful" reason: The fruit brings life, not death, she says, repeating Satan's words and using the serpent as the basis of her delusion that her eyes are now opened. She lies again in claiming that she has eaten for Adam's sake (877–78).

In a beautiful addition to the traditional story, as Adam hears of her trespass, his garland of roses drops, "faded," the first sign of death in Eden and a sign of Eve's innocence destroyed. In his sad but calm response, Adam sees that she, a gatherer of flowers, is "deflow'r'd" and doomed; rather than scold her, the shocked man at once sees that he too is ruined. Some readers have found his resignation to die with Eve (906–8) an indication of his own already fallen nature since his desire to defy God for her sake and his concern about being left alone seem surprisingly weak. But Adam knows that he is one with Eve (as no other man and woman can ever be) and, in his unfallen innocence, he is searching for hope. He recovers from his initial shock in the subsequent speech (921–59), suggesting his consideration of Eve's "Bold deed" and its seriousness, but he doubts that the penalty for disobeying will be death. In his love for her he believes the serpent's lies as he has heard them from Eve and presumes that God will not do what He said. Despite his angelic instruction, he cannot fathom evil, nor can he imagine losing Eve. In relying on his feelings rather than on reason, he places the natural bond higher than the law of God; as Eve reasons unwisely, he weakly follows his heart. His words reflect fear, selfishness, pride, and intemperance as well as an excessive desire for, and submissiveness to, Eve.

Milton wrote in *Christian Doctrine* that original sin contained a host of sins: distrust of divine truth, disbelief, ingratitude, gluttony, arrogance, deceit, sacrilege, presumption (in aspiring to the divine), fraud, uxoriousness in the man's worship of his wife, in the woman a lack of proper regard for her husband and offspring, as well as pride and disobedience.

Milton suspensefully delays the interval between the sin of Eve and that of her husband. Eve, glad to hear Adam's pledge of devotion, ironically calls it a "glorious trial of exceeding Love," words later applied to Christ, the Second Adam. Eve sees herself as a goddess and the fruit as a test of his love (975); she weeps for joy that he risks "Divine displeasure for her sake," and asserts that if she believed death would result, she would not persuade him to join her in eating. Yet death to her is a mere abstraction, never experienced, and she has replaced reason with imagined feelings. In eating "not deceiv'd" like Eve but foolishly "overcome with Female charm" (as if Satan has used Eve's beauty as a witch-like charm to overcome Adam), he sins against reason. Eating his fill, he chooses to follow his heart, oblivious to the second groan of Nature as the primal sin is complete. By eating of the tree of knowledge Adam and Eve become mortal and forego their chance to eat of the other tree—that of immortality. Intoxicated, they imagine themselves divine yet are debased: The only knowledge they receive from the tree of knowledge is that of lust.

Adam, delighting in his newly inflamed desire, thinks that the "delicious Fare" (with a pun on *fair*) makes Eve so beautiful that he must indulge his lustful appetite. Seizing her hand, he leads her to the bower, where they make love before awakening to a sense of "guilty shame"; their nakedness now signifies that they are bare of virtue and strength.

Fallen Adam scolds his wife, as he was not earlier wont to do, for he now angrily realizes that his eyes have been opened to evil. With a sense of remorse and fear, he cries out, wishing to hide from God because of his shame. Adam and Eve use leaves from the prolific trees to cover their genitals in sharp contrast with their innocent prelapsarian nakedness. So, too, their emotions grow turbulent and shake their "inward State of Mind" (1125), where reason no longer reigns. Adam blames her for disobeying him just as she will blame him, neither acknowledging that both have disobeyed God. Eve claims that their fall was inevitable, that

Fig. 3. Peter Paul Rubens (1577–1640), *The Fall*. Reproduced with permission of the Prado, Madrid.

Adam's rational superiority would have been unable to detect Satan's deception. When she accuses him of not being "firm," he blames her for his loss. Thus the book ends in mutual recrimination, the first marital battle reflecting the "Mistrust, Suspicion, Discord" caused by the sin.

## Book 10

Book 10 completes the climactic action of the poem by emphasizing Adam's progress from despair to humility and thus the triumph of love over hate. Not to include the events of this book with those of Book 9 is to devalue Milton's stress on reconciliation and to focus on the Fall and Satan, who cannot be seen as successful. The supreme irony of the epic is that man is not defeated, as Satan had thought. Like Book 3, which also opens with Heaven and moves to Sin and Death, this book is carefully structured, with Heaven, Hell, and Earth feeling the consequences of the Fall.

The "unwelcome news" of man's sin reaches Heaven, where God is not wrathful but comforting. He tells the assembled angels not to be dismayed by man's free choice since He will send the Son, a "mild Judge and Intercessor," not only to sentence but ultimately to redeem man. The Son promises to temper Justice with Mercy to satisfy the Father. As Milton wrote in the *Christian Doctrine,* Christ "voluntarily performed, and continues to perform, on behalf of man, whatever is requisite for obtaining reconciliation with God, and eternal salvation."

The Son comes to Eden in the cool evening, yet the time of repose for Adam and Eve is upset. They hear God call Adam, as in Genesis 3.9, and they are afraid and ashamed. Adam reluctantly blames Eve for his sin; since she seemed so perfect, he says, he could not believe she could do evil. The Son tells Adam that Eve's beauty was to lead him to love, not subjection. When the Judge asks the woman what she has done, her humble response is the single line from Genesis: "The serpent me beguil'd and I did eat." God's curse falls first on the serpent and leads to the mysterious oracle (179–81) prophesying one who would bruise the serpent's head; the Christian implications of this oracle will become clearer to Adam in Book 12. The Judge is also "Savior" who will assume "the form of Servant." Pitying Adam and Eve, he covers both their physical and their "inward nakedness."

Meanwhile Sin and Death, seated at the wide gates of Hell, feel newly strengthened because of Satan's "success." Sin proposes that a monument be erected of "merit high," the perverted use of *merit* again reminding the Christian reader of the merits of the cross (as, for example, at 12.409). Death, smelling the "mortal carnage" on Earth, eagerly agrees that a highway between Hell and Earth be built. In a parody of the divine creating Spirit (1.9, 7.233), they hover "upon the waters" and collect soil that Death then turns to stone, completing a vast bridge. Hell is thus firmly cemented to our now defenseless world. As Satan returns to his family disguised as an angel, Milton tells us that, after the temptation of Eve, the serpent had slipped away unnoticed, changed his shape, and watched the effects of his seduction before fleeing in fear from the divine Judge. He returned at night to learn both the plight of Adam and Eve and his own "doom," which he interpreted as having a future application. Thus "with joy" he returns to view the bridge and is greeted by Sin, who notes the strengthened union between Satan, Sin and Death, parallel to the bond between Adam and Eve. Her speech of praise makes Satan's epic antiheroism complete. She believes that Satan has "fully avenged" their heavenly foe, but Satan's courage has not wounded God but man. Satan, proud of his "glorious Work" in linking Hell with the universe, glories in the literal meaning of "Satan" (adversary) but has failed to be God's antagonist, as he claims. As he returns to Hell, his offspring are to descend to paradise to rule as his ordained deputies; these grand orders ironically recall God's authorization of Adam and Eve as lords over creation as well as language used in giving consuls supreme power to protect ancient Rome against injury in time of crisis.[40]

Satan passes through the unguarded gate of Hell, the demons having gone to Pandemonium to await his return. Like Odysseus returning to Ithaca, Satan enters the hall disguised so that his sudden discovery by the Grand Council will be all the more glorious, pointing up his imagined role as epic sojourner. The Peers, joyfully greeting Satan, are silenced as he delivers his final speech. As preposterous as Satan's claim to lead them out of Hell is his insistence that he has made them "Lords" of the new world by his great adventure, thereby restoring their old titles to them.

Equally false is his boast that he overcame the opposition of Night and Chaos. And he scornfully attributes man's fall to a mere apple, contending that God has given up on human life. A final lie is that the serpent, not Satan, was sentenced—and to a mere bruise. Who would not "purchase" (a word often associated with the Redemption) a world at such a minor cost? he asks, urging his cohorts to rise. Instead, surprised to hear a "universal hiss," he finds himself cast down ("supplanted") into the form of a serpent, punished by losing the very power of speech that he has used to glorify himself and seduce Eve. The analogous monsters and reptiles Milton cites add both to the horror of the scene and to the onomatopoetic applause of hissing; the other demons, expecting Satan's triumph as they wait outside Pandemonium, are also cast down in fitting punishment.

In an interesting allegorical addition that Milton uses to relate Hell and Eden, the devils' penance is aggravated by a grove of hellish trees, which tantalize the devils with enticing fruit that deceives the taste so that they eat "bitter Ashes." As Sin takes up full-time residence in paradise, followed by Death with his insatiable appetite, God, seeing these "Dogs of Hell" setting out to wreak havoc on the world, and says that His enemies should not think He has given up His creation to "their misrule"; God announces the triumph of good over evil (634–40). These lines reflect Milton's faith in what he described as a "new heaven and a new earth . . . coming down from God" and in "the destruction of the present unclean and polluted world."

Seasonal changes occur, and discord in nature manifests itself in the hostility among animals. Seeing this misery, Adam, in his long soliloquy (720–844) of lament and despair, faces his greatest postlapsarian crisis: how to cope with his new guilt, fear, and alienation from God. Alone, he wrestles with a host of feelings ranging from doubt, grief, and resentment to fear and horror; like the hero in *Samson Agonistes,* he undergoes a process of self-discovery and regeneration, moving beyond pride and despair to acknowledge his guilt and receive Eve as a partner in his sin and reconciliation. The contrast between his former innocence and his present shame is captured in the initial paradox, "O miserable of happy!" He curses the fact of his creation, not his Creator, whose justice he questions. He then realizes that it is too late to reject the terms of his creation or contest the joys he was given; but his reasoning is again overcome by fears: Will I undergo a living death or be annihilated? Will death end the torment, or is my spirit imperishable? Such questions indicate that Adam's mind is struggling to reassert itself, and they reveal the need for the further education of Books 11 and 12, where, aided by Michael's instruction, he will learn to trust in God's mercy.

Adam reasons (804–8) that an infinite God need not exact infinite punishment, but fear returns as well as the feeling that death might be eternal and that in him all posterity "stands curst." He finally absolves God of injustice and accepts his own guilt (831), thus undergoing the first of the four steps in regeneration cited in Milton's *Christian Doctrine:* "conviction of sin, contrition, confession, departure from evil and conversion to good." Though he sees no way out of the horrors into which his introspection has led him, Adam has made an important beginning in the process of repentance.

As he laments, Adam lies on the cold ground, no longer erect but prone, like the serpent (9.497) or like the newly fallen Satan in Book 1 (195). He longs for death, whose stroke would be "thrice acceptable" in ending his misery, satisfying the demands of truth, and fulfilling divine justice. Eve watches his passionate mourning, but he angrily dismisses her with curses, irrationally blaming his wife for rejecting his warning and for being taken in by the serpent as he was taken in by Eve. He stops attacking her only long enough to question God's creation of woman, whose "snares" will supposedly lead to more evils.

Eve is too strong to be repelled by Adam's wrath, and her selfless plea for peace makes his selfish wailing look foolish. It is apt that she who began the Fall by upsetting the sexual hierarchy should begin the process of restoration by returning to her female role as the nurturing source of harmony and love. With tears and humility she begs Adam not to abandon her, not to deprive her of guidance, for as they sinned together, so must they live, hostile only to the serpent. She sees herself as more miserable than Adam, for she has sinned against both God and Adam (931) and cries that God might punish her alone.

Though he warns her not to undertake the joint burden of punishment, Adam is moved by Eve's sincere, humble pleas. His love for her is such that he would have all guilt "visited" on him. Rather than blame each other, he concludes, let us see how together we can share our grief. Now reconciled with Adam and "hopeful to regain" his full love, Eve confides certain disturbing thoughts (childlessness, suicide) about ways to reduce or end their misery. Eve's "contempt of life" (1013) is contrary to her maternal, feminine role; she wishes to overturn the divine command to increase and multiply. Her proposal "to destroy destruction by self-destruction is a parodic perversion of the Son's readiness to defeat death by dying."[41]

Continuing to forge the proper path in the face of an uncertain future, Adam urges Eve away from self-destruction, which he sees as marring her excellence; death, he says, is an unavoidable penalty. He recognizes that he broke faith with God by disobeying and by ignoring the welfare of his offspring; he will not, as Eve is willing to do, repeat the sin. This is an important turning point for Adam in resolving the crisis. Adam's heroism requires that he choose obedience over violence, humility over selfishness, hope over despair. He expects to find comfort in labor and recalls that Eve's childbearing will be joyful as well as painful. The "Fruit of thy Womb" (1053) reminds us that Mary, the second Eve, and her Son, the second Adam, will be descendants of the old Adam and Eve, whose sinful fruit will result in a new kind of fruitfulness. He recognizes, aided by divine grace, that prayer will sustain them in coping with Eden's changes and that God will comfort them so they "need not fear" to live out their lives. Aware that God's judgment is based on love, Adam advocates trust and prayer: they must humbly confess their sins, "with tears / Watering the ground," contrite lines repeated as the book ends.

## Book 11

Although the conclusion of *Paradise Lost* has been criticized as disappointing and inartistic, its plainer style well suits Milton's purpose: to explain how the "paradise within" will far surpass that of the garden in Eden. Such a purpose does not require a grand or resonant style. As G. K. Hunter observes, since the narrator of the final books tries to define human existence in relation both to the Fall and to the Second Coming, the feeling is one of sorrow mixed with joy as griefs are balanced by consolation.[42] The last two books are important since the reader's knowledge of postlapsarian history cannot be greater than Adam's.[43] As the poem's principal character, Adam must complete his education in virtue and understand God's plan of salvation in a way that reveals his patient heroism. Though necessarily didactic, Books 11 and 12 satisfy the reader as to Adam's emotional, spiritual, and intellectual progress and state of mind. Despite the lack of a continuous narrative connecting the Expulsion with the Incarnation, the series of selected episodes effectively conveys Adam's step-by-step learning process. The condensed historical panorama of these books leads not to an unknown future, but to the real world where Adam and the reader can learn that sin results in the need for the Redemption and individual righteousness. Milton, with his firm sense of structure, establishes a parallel between the last two books, depicting fallen man, and the first two, depicting the fallen angels.

That Adam and Eve will cover their one bad deed with good ones is not to excuse them from the Fall but to emphasize Adam's new set of options and moral lessons. The many stages of history that pass in review show the possibilities for exercising choice. The panorama of time "gives the setting in which the individual must perpetually repair injustice. . . . How the individual may act upon the flow of history is the subject of the epic, which gives to the poem its intellectual force." [44]

Adam and Eve remain in the prayerful posture of Book 10, aided by God's "Prevenient Grace," that is, strengthened in advance by divine power, which has removed the hardness of their hearts. As representatives of the human race, they are compared to Deucalion and Pyrrha, who, having survived Jupiter's punitive flood, asked Themis, the goddess of justice, how lost mankind could be restored. The Son as the Word of God articulates man's silent prayer in lines recalling 1 John 2.1–2 (Christ is the advocate, "the propitiation of our sins"), asking that his own merit fulfill man's good deeds just as his death will atone for man's evil deeds. Thus the death penalty is not removed but mitigated since God will die as man, who will die to a new life with God. God will "remove" man from paradise, not harshly expel him, since he cannot eat of the Tree of Life and live on earth forever.

At dawn, after a night of prayer, Adam and Eve find new strength and hope. Adam feels God's gentle presence through his prayer and recalls the promise that Eve's descendants will bruise the foe. But then the eagle and the lion turn into hunters as the sky darkens, and Adam sees in these signs portents of uncertainty: How long, he wonders, will the death penalty be delayed? Michael, dressed as a man in armor, comes to allay such fears and to announce that God has heard their prayers, death will be ultimately defeated, time for repentance is allowed, but remaining in the garden is not permitted. Adam is stunned by this unexpected news, and Eve, overhearing, cries out in anguish. In a beautiful lament for the only world she has known, she shows herself overly attached to the senses; for her to be banished from paradise is worse than death. Michael reminds her to be patient, to recall that earthly goods are but lent to man, and that to be with her husband should be adequate solace.

When Adam humbly accepts his expulsion and laments the loss of God's friendship, Michael assures him that leaving the garden does not entail leaving God. To strengthen Adam's faith in the signs of God's goodness, Michael will reveal the future to him so that he will learn patience, the key to Adam's education. In his inner struggle between joy and sorrow, he is to learn spiritual fortitude. As he oscillates between hope and despair, naively rushing to judge each vision Michael presents, Adam is gradually educated and his responses corrected. Unlike the closed minds of the devils, his attitude is open; he is eager to progress from error to insight. This process of discovery, a paradigm of slow progress in history, is a patient search for God's presence in the fallen world. Along with the external biblical history that Michael presents, Adam learns in response to the contrasts he sees between unbearable evil and the seemingly pleasant goods that lead to complacency. As Hunter observes, "Adam is tempted through his responses to death, to secular peace, and to power," the emphasis falling more on his feelings than on historical facts.[45]

Ascending the hill of revelation while Eve sleeps, Adam awakes to a new understanding of the future, with its promise of redemptive hope. This vision has epic as well as biblical precedents, recalling the vision of Rome's future seen by Aeneas (*Aeneid* 6.754–854), Daniel's vision of Michael coming to the aid of exiled Israel (Daniel 10.13), the prophet Ezekiel's visions of God (Ezekiel 10.2), and the devil's temptation of Christ on a high mountain (Matthew 4.8); climbing the high hill also suggests the ascent of Calvary by the second Adam. From such a lofty place, Adam can see virtually all the world's kingdoms. Michael clears

Adam's vision, darkened by sin, and sharpens the eyes of his mind as Adam enters a trance.

He opens his eyes to three disturbing visions of the violent effects of his sin: Cain's murder of Abel, followed by scenes of disease; wantonness among Cain's descendants, including the specious nature of worldly pleasure; and the "brazen Throat of War," including Milton's critique of the classical ideal of valor. Adam then weeps to see the Flood (738–53) until he is told that, amid the evils of every age, one just man, such as Noah (Genesis 6.14–22), will rise to demonstrate God's Providence. The Flood is the center of Milton's narrative and the rainbow a hopeful sign of God's new covenant. The vignettes of Book 11, with their alternating revelations of destruction and corruption, indicate that God's purpose is not constantly evident in human life. After the Flood, the covenant provides an explicit thread of continuity for the subsequent events of the epic.[46]

## Book 12

In the final book, the pictorial series of visions is replaced by didactic narrative, as befits an epic of explanation. Since Michael's presentation of the future results in the knowledge necessary for salvation, it must rely on precept as well as example. Though Milton's selection and summary of biblical history are generally well handled and thematically apt, the static, undramatic tone of Book 12 has disturbed some readers, who find Michael's long, uninterrupted speech to Adam (80–265) an example of poetically arid verse. For the poet, who divided the tenth book of the first edition of *Paradise Lost* to form the eleventh and twelfth books of the present, second edition, the change to oral narration was no doubt necessitated by the constraints of space. He does not attempt an inclusive survey of the Old Testament but selects episodes that will help Adam in his growth in patient fortitude. Adam, whose name means *man,* is a symbolic everyman whose sin is everyone's, just as his reconciliation is universal; thus he and Milton's intended readers must learn Christian principles if the poet's purpose (to justify the ways of God) is to be fulfilled. As Milton wrote in the *Christian Doctrine,* human regeneration is made possible by the Redemption, but the Christian must willingly undergo suffering after the manner of Christ. This is the truth that Adam learns to accept by the end of the epic.

Christ as the ideal embodiment of Milton's patient heroism was revealed during Raphael's account of the war in Heaven (6.710–893); Michael's narrative now completes Adam's education by relating the theme of love and obedience to the Son. Messiah's victories on the cross and at the end of time were mysteriously prophesied to Adam in the oracle of Book 10 (179–81); the full meaning of this oracle becomes clear in Book 12. This gradual revelation provides necessary links between the infinite heroism of Messiah, portrayed in glory at the end of time (12.451–65), and the finite heroism of Adam as he responds to what the future will entail. As such, the final book connects the fall of Satan and the fall of Adam with the emergence of the Son as hero. Milton also prepares the reader to see that the Second Coming is not to be a war (as in the Book of Revelation) but the inner acceptance of Christ, making possible the "paradise within." Adam's freely chosen submission to love becomes the proper response to the panorama of history's evils in Book 11 and to the story of faithfulness from Abraham to Moses in 12. Milton's intention to sing of "the better fortitude / Of Patience and Heroic Martyrdom" (9.31–32) is fulfilled in Adam, Enoch, Noah, Abraham, Moses, and, finally Christ, whose endurance reflects the love of God for man.

Michael's narrative concerns the story of the Chosen People after the Flood and emphasizes the key Miltonic theme of liberty and its loss due to sin, which obscures the reason and thereby causes political disorder. The Laws given to Moses on Mount Sinai are seen as foreshadowing the New Covenant, for Moses is a type of Christ as mediator, the "destin'd Seed" (233) who will bruise the serpent. When Adam asks why laws are needed for a blessed people, he is told that laws cannot prevent the sins of his descendants. Michael's speech (285–99) reflects the Calvinist position that, given the essential corruption of man, grace is essential for salvation. Salvation comes through righteousness whereby man's corrupt nature can be "covered" by grace and made presentable to God, as Milton makes clear in specifying the "Robe of righteousness" with which the Son clothes Adam and Eve (10.220–23). But Milton rejects the Calvinist view that grace is bestowed arbitrarily since this requires a belief in predestination.

The blood sacrifices of the Hebrews are seen as "shadows or types of Christ's expiation of sin";[47] thus the old covenant between God and man will lead to a "better Cov'nant" (302), through which faith, not law, produces true righteousness.

While foreshadowings of the Redemption as the means of God's deliverance continue, Adam is told that the prophesied bruise will not destroy Satan but his legacy of sin and death. Since the penalty (death) for Adam's disobedience can only be paid or redeemed by death and since no one can satisfy God's justice but God, atonement can only be made by the Son of God (outlined in 3.294–97). This act will bruise Satan's head by crushing his strength (430), thereby revealing the full meaning of the prophecy given to Adam in Book 10.

Adam, in recognizing that a greater good will come from evil, states the central theme of the fortunate fall: without Adam's sin, there would be no eternal salvation through Christ. Unsure whether to repent or rejoice, Adam expresses the mixed feelings of the entire poem. Paradise is lost, but God's goodness will result in a new happiness for man.

Michael speaks of the Holy Spirit, who will guide the church after Christ's Ascension and arm his followers with grace. But in Milton's condensed version of Christian history, colored by his clerical antipathy and frustration over reform, faith and truth will be rare until the end of time when the Son in glory will destroy evil.

Adam's final speech reveals that he has discovered the meaning of obedience and love, which are embodied in the patient heroism of Christ's redemptive action: "suffering for Truth's sake / Is fortitude to highest victory" (659–70). Adam's acceptance of the Redemption, which makes possible his regeneration (12.469–73), signifies the spiritual strength that his education in virtue has produced. Michael, who is (unlike Raphael) divinely inspired (11.115), notes that Adam has attained to the sum of wisdom by realizing the redemptive value of suffering. Adam has attained the state of mind intended by God when He ordered Michael to send Adam from Eden "sorrowing yet in peace" (11.117), for he has learned of that "one greater Man" (1.4).

Michael is a prophet of "utmost hope" for Adam and Milton's intended readers, for he defines the "paradise within," made possible by the chief Christian virtue, love, that will make humankind "happier far" than the earthly paradise. Real time replaces prophetic vision as Adam and Michael descend the hill to awaken Eve. Prompted by dreams that have forecast "some great good," she is reconciled to the future and is ready to follow Adam. The last words are Eve's and reflect the comforting hope of the Redemption: She recognizes that her sin has lost Eden but knows that through her the "Promis'd Seed shall all restore." With these words of consolation, Adam and Eve end their stay in Eden, willingly reconciled to trust in what Providence will unfold, comforted to know that the deliverer will be among their offspring.

As Eden turns into a blazing wilderness, the angel takes their hands, gently leading them out into the world, but not wrathfully so, as in most visual renderings of the expulsion. The ending of *Paradise Lost* is neither harsh nor pessimistic, nor does it, as some critics suggest, show signs of the poet's failing skills. The epic ends with the first steps in humanity's long wandering journey from innocence to experience. Milton's subdued conclusion conveys a perfect blending of hope and melancholy, joy and sorrow as Adam and Eve, "hand in hand" and guided by God, undertake their uncertain journey. Their sorrow for a paradise lost is more than balanced with hope for a better world to come.

# 4

# "A Life Heroic": *Paradise Regained* and *Samson Agonistes*

Milton's final two poems, published together in 1671, concern Christian heroism and the themes of temptation, obedience, and the "truest fortitude" of patience. *Paradise Regained,* a philosophical poem in four books, depicts Christ's emergence as the exemplar of ideal heroism through his temptation in the desert by Satan. *Samson Agonistes,* a Christian version of Greek tragedy, is a powerful dramatization of inner regeneration based on the familiar biblical story. Milton's "brief epic" seems to have been written between 1667 and 1671. Although some scholars have argued for a much earlier date for the tragedy, it has traditionally been considered the poet's final achievement. The two poems, planned to complement each other and to complete *Paradise Lost,* illustrate virtues associated with Christ and needed by mankind to uncover the "paradise within." Choosing to respond patiently to evil is a theme developed, not in the longer epic, but in these two related works, which make explicit Michael's lesson to Adam (*Paradise Lost,* 12.575–87) about cultivating internal heroism.

Milton's publication of these two poems in one volume is not accidental. John T. Shawcross shows the complementary nature of the works: "We see in Samson what the Son as Man could have become had he succumbed to any of the temptations of Satan, and in the Son we see what Samson as the 'great Deliverer'—the ironic earthly counterpart of the true 'heavenly' deliverer—should have been."[1] Both works show how the message in *Paradise Lost* about cultivating the heroism of virtue can be realized, and they reflect Milton's belief that the individual, not just institutions, must be changed if society is to be improved. These two final poems also indicate something of the poet's hopeful attitude at the end of his life. Unlike the political leaders of the 1650s, the Son of God and Samson, apparent failures in their own time, faced temptations and triumphed. Samson's destruction of the Philistines and the Son's victory over Satan reveal possibilities not realized in history, suggesting the hope that the people of England might one day succeed. For Milton, the cause for which he fought remained viable; only its leaders had gone astray. Samson, the chosen leader of a minority who was to deliver Israel from bondage, can be seen as the protagonist of a dramatic poem about national failure and political patience. If Milton in *Samson* condemns "the clergy and aristocracy whom he regarded as the principal enemies of God in restoration England,"[2] the counterparts of the Philistine leaders are those who returned England to the apostasy that had, for Milton, so long frustrated Christianity. To end this apostasy and prepare for the millennium was heroic in the eyes of the poet, who believed that what had once been overthrown could be overthrown again. According to this reading, Milton in his final poems remains a man of hope amid the experience of defeat who awaits the fulfillment on earth of messianic Christianity.

## *Paradise Regained*

In *Paradise Regained,* Milton shows Jesus resisting Satan's temptations, as recounted in Luke 4.1–13. Whereas Adam and Eve succumbed to temptation, losing Paradise, the Second Adam regained it by his victory over Satan. As the opening indicates, the poet, inspired by the same Spirit as in the earlier epic, now sings of the recovery of Paradise by "one man's firm obedience fully tried / Through all temptation." The words of Paul (Romans 5.19) were no doubt in the poet's mind as he conceived *Paradise Regained:* "as by one man's disobedience many were made sinners, so by the obedience of one shall many be made righteous." Milton, then, created two epic poems on Paradise and temptation, the second on a smaller scale.

Readers expecting a description of the Passion or Resurrection and the chance to see Satan sent back to Hell will be disappointed with the choice of subject: How, they might ask, is Paradise regained in this poetic debate between Christ and Satan? As *Paradise Lost* (12.393–97) makes clear, the Savior, by love and by obedience to the law, will redeem man's sin "Not by destroying Satan, but his works." As Reformation doctrine familiar to Milton emphasized, the Redemption included much more than the Passion; its lesson involved Christ's active obedience to God's will and his passive obedience on the Cross, the latter redeeming sin and the former recovering eternal life.[3] The Son's triumph at the end of *Paradise Regained* allows him to begin the salvation of humankind by raising the fallen descendants of Adam to Paradise, which is not a place but a state signifying man's eternal life with God.

Milton's idea of the brief epic is modeled on the Book of Job.[4] Because of his wisdom and patient endurance, Job was seen as prefiguring Christ in being tempted and seemingly abandoned by God. Milton, emphasizing obedience and patience, develops in the poem his idea of Christian heroism through the issues of temptation and choice. Christ's growth toward full understanding of himself and his redemptive mission arises out of his being tempted. Themes of identity and self-knowledge are also central in the poem: by demonstrating an understanding of himself as Messiah, the Son is able to overcome Satan.

The action of the poem is largely internalized, and the vast epic scope of *Paradise Lost* reduced, so that the poet's focus is concentrated on the struggle between good and evil, centered on a single, representative individual, who performs deeds "Above Heroic." The Son's growth in self-knowledge constitutes the poem's inner struggle, which is seen as superior to external conflicts involving physical valor. Although Jesus is a perfect man, far abler to resist Satan than was Job, the poet emphasizes the humanity of his hero. Although the perfect hero is free from direct Satanic attack, he is not free of human doubts and fears. The poet is skillful in making the strong Son seem doubtful and the weak Satan seem assertive.[5] Satan is never the evenly matched adversary of the Son but a desperate, if still clever, spokesman for worldly wisdom who moves from assurance to fear while the Son moves from doubt to certainty. The reader's uncertainty about the ways in which the exaltation of the Messiah, described in the opening of the poem, will be effected constitutes the poem's human interest.

*Paradise Regained* has been considered static and undramatic since the Son cannot lose nor Satan win, yet there is a genuine dramatic encounter in the poem, as Barbara Lewalski shows.[6] The choices involved are real: the Son's chosen rejection of the tempter and his acceptance of God gain the inner Paradise. Moreover, as in *Paradise Lost,* the heavenly begetting of the Son and his future victory over sin and death are inherently dramatic. Still, as Michael warns Adam (in *Paradise Lost,* 12.386–88), the Son and Satan will not fight a literal battle; thus the reader is prepared for an action involving internal struggle and an emerging awareness of the protagonist's identity. And one must share in the Son's temporary passivity as he waits patiently for the fulfillment of God's will. Like Samson, the Son has a growing awareness of his public mission that is not apparent in the external action. The poem's action is essentially intellectual, its intensity arising from the opposition of ideas and wills, from the contrast, as Jon Lawry says, between the promise at Jordan of a union between man and God and the loss associated with the desert, which will ultimately bloom into a greater Paradise than the earthly Eden. To Satan, the revelation at Jordan means that the Son will be a literal king, an earthly rival, not his spiritual adversary. Thus the Devil wants the Son to demand his promised kingdom, paradoxically assuring its fall, whereas the Son, by accepting the solitude of the desert, assures that the promises of Jordan will be fulfilled.[7]

Critics have noted the vague, dreamlike quality of *Paradise Regained,* its sudden shifts between waking and dreaming, its abrupt transitions, its hero's silence and waiting. Since, from the poem's Christian perspective, speech and action demonstrate pride, the patient, dispassionate Son, in moving toward ideal obedience, chooses silence over words. Whereas Satan is rhetorically dazzling, the Son is restrained, terse, poised, self-controlled, avoiding any self-indulgence. Language becomes associated with the false appeals of Satan, who relishes rhetoric while the Son scorns it. Decorum required Milton to use a plain style for the Son, whose quiet, understated language resembles that of Scripture. In using private rather than public language and in choosing simplicity and silence rather than showy elaboration, the Son rejects the worldly values of language, seeing (at 4.171) that Satan's "abominable" talk serves the purposes of the self rather than advancing God's kingdom.[8]

In defeating Satan with intelligence rather than weapons, Christ displays a mastery of self that becomes more important than his mastery of arms. Rather than developing his physical valor, Christ has studied the word of God, thus sharpening his skill in confronting his adversary. It is, he says, "more humane, more heavenly" to use "winning words" rather than weapons (1.221–22) to persuade those with "willing hearts" to accept the good and to reject evil, thereby defeating the tempter. Christ thus exemplifies Milton's ideal of magnanimity by balancing action and contemplation. Since God has commanded that the Redemption be effected by a man who will be tried, die, and rise again to Heaven, Christ fulfills the divine will, and his fortitude is his patience in the face of temptation.[9] Like Samson, he combines active and passive heroism, choosing to obey and suffer as a sacrificial victim, rejecting the older ideal of courage based on pride or honor. In resisting Satan's temptations, the ascetic hero also exercises the virtue of temperance. He responds with patient words to the attempt (3.176) to persuade him to liberate the people of Israel before such action is sanctioned by God: "All things are best fulfilled in their due time." The Son sacrifices his own will to that of the Father and refuses to declare his independence of God, as Satan tries to get him to do. This renunciation of self is reflected in the passivity of the Son, who rejects the Satanic assertion of self. Christ's strength is revealed by apparent weakness, his power by inaction. Such responses frustrate Satan, who is unable to find out who Christ is, to change the course of events, to do more than set the scene for what he hopes might be dramatic or revealing confrontations. He urges the Son to fulfill the words of the prophets by seizing opportunity, not by waiting; he thus challenges the very patient heroism the Son embodies. While responding that his prophesied mission will be fulfilled in God's own time, the Son reflects on the reason for the delay: his obedience is being tried, and he must learn to suffer and obey before learning to rule: "who best / Can suffer, best can do" (3.195–96). The reader, knowing Christ's identity and redemptive action, is in a stronger position than Satan and sees what the Adversary cannot: the Son's gradual self-realization and increasing confidence; this leads the reader to reject Satan's perception of the Son's passivity as weakness.

In a nontraditional, nonscriptural attack on human learning (4.285–364), Milton has the Son disdain the study of human wisdom since it may not lead to knowledge of self and God but only glorify the self. This controversial rejection of the humanistic learning prized by the poet, rather than reflecting Milton's aged disillusionment, comes at a climactic moment in the Son's gradual development of his identity. As Rajan says, the reader ironically sees, as Satan cannot, that Christ must refuse the learning of Athens in order to declare his true, historic identity, which transcends "Nature's light" (228). "If the light of nature is to be redeemed by the light of grace, if the law is to culminate in the gospel, he who brings the higher wisdom into history can scarcely accept the lower as a substitute."[10] Thus, tempted to exchange classical learning for revelation, Christ must choose the latter. Even for Milton the humanist, the value of secular culture can never be equivalent to that of Christianity. For the reader attentive to the role of Christ as redeemer and judge, the Son's dismissal of pagan philosophy is in keeping with his spiritual mission to restore the fallen world of nature.

At the climax of his efforts to determine the Son's identity and in response to the Son's demonstrated moral perfection, Satan seizes him, carrying him through the air to the topmost pinnacle of the temple in Jerusalem, ordering him to stand or cast himself down; for if he is the Son of God, the Father will save him. The Son's simple, ambiguous response is the climax of this dramatic confrontation: "Tempt not the Lord thy God." Does Jesus mean, "Do not tempt God, who I am," or "To do as you say, I would tempt God's providence"? Some critics have seen both responses as possible: Christ establishes his divinity and simultaneously makes his supreme act of trust and obedience. In this line, the Son both warns Satan of the Father's wrath and presents himself as the Father's perfect image. As Rajan says, the Son reaches the pinnacle of his own identity at the very moment that Satan is reminded of his earlier failure.[11] In a brilliantly rendered climactic moment, Satan falls while the Son stands. The adversary falls with "amazement," seeing that he has unwittingly reenacted his old battle with the Son of God, whom he now recognizes as the heavenly victor of the War in Heaven. Thus, in this interpretation, Satan realizes that his enemy will always be the same, and the reader is reminded of his defeat at the end of time.

Christ's use of free will to choose what is morally right has been a symbolic reversal of Adam's Fall. With the rule of Satan and his cohorts ended, the Devil will henceforth dread the Son, who will now "begin to save mankind." As in *Paradise Lost,* the ending is a beginning; its quiet conclusion points up the conflict between private virtue and public ambition and contrasts with the theatrical display staged by Satan, whose thunder has been silenced.

Although Milton drew upon the Book of Job, *The Faerie Queene* (2.8), and Giles Fletcher's *Christ's Victorie and Triumph in Heaven and Earth,* among other sources, *Paradise Regained* is original in conception and consistent in tone. The poet preferred the later poem to *Paradise Lost,* though few readers have agreed, some disliking the remote character of Christ or criticizing its limited scope and didactic tone. Since Milton's epic goals, cited in *Paradise Lost* 9.25–41, were not completed in that poem, *Paradise Regained* may be seen as another attempt to define Christian heroism. Milton's lifelong view of man as an integrated spiritual and physical whole is reflected in his perfect hero. The effort to assimilate the Christ of the Gospels with a heroic ideal of magnanimity may have been the poet's greatest artistic challenge, one increasingly seen by critics as successful.

If, according to the mythic subtext of *Paradise Regained,* the wilderness of temptation symbolizes life itself, the poem can be seen as representing the individual's ideal passage through life to salvation. The Son, then, represents Man, whose humanity exists "in conjunction with the sense of the divine within him."[12] The poem makes explicit the final message of the longer epic—that the internal heroism of patient fortitude, along with faith, temperance and love, will help one find the "paradise within." The lesson of hopefulness for humankind in the brief epic helps explain Milton's preference for this poem, Shawcross suggests, and it suits Milton's belief in a "religion of one," in salvation as individualistic, since the complete victory over evil will only come from the inner strength of the individual. The philosophical basis of *Paradise Regained* is the ability of individuals to fashion their own worth, actively moving toward God by their unaided effort so that God will assist them in coping with adversities.

## *Samson Agonistes*

Sometimes called Milton's most perfect poem, *Samson Agonistes* has an intensity of feeling that sets it apart from the poet's other works. It succeeds in being both a "classical" tragedy and a religious drama exemplifying Milton's ideal of Christian heroism. Critics have not always agreed about its greatness, however, contending that the Greek tragedy and biblical story do not form a harmonious whole or that, as a play, it lacks dramatic conflict. But the apparent lack of action in *Samson* is due to its emphasis on the unseen regeneration of the hero. Milton's subject is intellectual and psychological change and growth from self-destruction to rebirth.

Most scholars find it impossible to date *Samson* before the poet's blindness or even before the Restoration (1660) since there are some inescapable parallels between Milton's frustration, sorrow, and bitterness and the feelings of Samson, "blind, dishearten'd, sham'd" among his enemies. The story of Samson, from the Old Testament (Book of Judges) provided Milton not merely with personal parallels but with material for a drama that could express both active, Greek heroism and passive, Christian suffering in an emotionally and intellectually demanding way. Milton again explores the theme that Providence guides and sustains the righteous, and he experiments both with the nature of tragedy and with verse that is more irregular and colloquial than in either epic. Milton also expresses in *Samson* his political vision. Since he saw in the biblical record of God's past dealings with man the pattern of His present dealings, the poet found in the Samson story a means of lamenting England's failure to establish God's law. *Samson* can be seen, then, as a political and prophetic work in which the destiny of Samson corresponds to that of England.[13]

In the Bible Samson revealed the secret of his God-given strength to Dalila and thus betrayed himself and his people, the Israelites, to their Philistine enemies. Blinded and taken captive by the Philistines, Samson, once a mighty hero, was reduced to the status of a slave before he redeemed his people at the pagan festival honoring the Philistine god, Dagon, fulfilling his destiny by pulling down the temple on his nation's enemies and killing himself in the process. Milton prepares for this final action, which occurs offstage, by presenting a series of exchanges, first between

Samson and the Chorus of Danites, then with the hero's father, Manoa, then with his second wife, Dalila, and finally with the bragging challenger, Harapha. As a result, he works his way through his shame and despair to enact what he perceives to be God's will. Although Milton declared that his work "never was intended" for the stage, it can be read as a drama in five "acts":

Lines 1–329: Samson alone and with the Chorus
330–724: Samson and Manoa
725–1061: Samson and Dalila
1062–1444: Samson with Harapha and Officer
1445–1758: Samson in temple (offstage)

The relentless focus of the drama is on Samson. He begins at a point where most tragic protagonists end, for the play, with its emphasis on the hero's enlightenment, reverses the traditional Aristotelian movement from good to bad. Milton's preface to *Samson* starts with the principle of catharsis since the poet believed that tragic beauty comes from the suffering and triumphant death of the protagonist, whose regeneration must be dominant.[14] In combining classical form and Christian meaning, the poet also asserted that tragedy should end on a note of reconciliation and harmony. Unable to change the story, he could lead up to and prepare for Samson's final deed in his own way. He chose an action that provides the hero with the spiritual fortitude necessary to be a suffering martyr, an action that also goads him out of his despair so that he can resume his former valor. In one ironic action, Samson makes a final ransom for his sin and is given the chance to achieve his purpose in life. He is thus both rewarded and punished. In the triumphant catastrophe, Samson combines active with passive heroism, both bravely doing and patiently suffering.

Milton exploits numerous ironies in developing the biblical story into a Christian tragedy: the hero's special relation to God makes him a social outcast; his movement toward spiritual regeneration is simultaneously a movement toward catastrophe; he is an enslaved deliverer, victorious in defeat, whose descent into darkness is also an ascent into illumination. At the end of the play, he is at the lowest as well as at the highest point of his life, fulfilling his destiny by slaying while also being slain. Milton makes the hero's way back to God lead to catastrophe so that the irony is "at once compatible with the Christian outlook and as potent as any to be found in tragedy anywhere."[15] The play can be seen, then, as both tragic and Christian; the hero, though aided by God, chooses to act in accordance with the divine will. Samson is depicted as the suffering hero, engaged in the conquest of himself; he is also the instrument of God's power, bringing divine judgment against his enemies. Samson's great suffering and death produce an effect of tragic waste and loss, similar to the pattern of Greek tragedy. Unlike Oedipus, however, Samson has not only sinned, been punished, and repented; he is also restored to God's service. His heroic ordeal, like that of the Son in *Paradise Regained,* reflects what Milton in the *Christian Doctrine* called the "good temptation" by which God tempts "even righteous men, in order to prove them . . . to exercise or demonstrate their faith or patience."

Milton's title refers to the Greek *agon* (struggle) as well as to the Pauline notion of the Christian warrior (Ephesians 6.11–18). The play uniquely blends Greek technique, Hebrew story, and Christian purpose. In its emphasis on tragic irony and catharsis, in its use of the Chorus, in its observing of the classical "unities" and other features, *Samson* seems Greek. In its concern with law, national destiny, vengeance, and justice, it seems Hebraic. In its theme of vicarious sacrifice and human dignity in the face of suffering and degradation, it is Christian. Christ's obedience to the Father redeems Adam's disobedience; so, too, the obedience of Samson can redeem the effect of his earlier sin. But, since he is so largely unaware of the meaning of his pain and public humiliation, Samson can only be seen as dimly foreshadowing, not imitating, Christ. He is a faithful champion of God who achieves revenge and fame rather than eternal life in Heaven; he is not a savior who forgives and redeems.[16] Since Samson ultimately obeys the spirit rather than the letter of the law, his action can perhaps be said to prefigure Christian liberty, which means, in Milton's words, that "Christ our liberator frees us from the slavery of sin and from the rule of the law, and of men."

The action, starting well after Samson's sin and enslavement, begins in early morning and will end in a "blaze of noon." The hero's emotional darkness contrasts with the symbolic light of life, faith, and spiritual insight. Though he has a sense of some new beginning, Samson finds no peace of mind from his "restless thoughts." In a long soliloquy, he wonders why his birth was foretold, why he was "Destin'd for great exploits," if he must die betrayed and scorned by his enemies. He laments that his special relationship with God has resulted in his being punished. The inner conflict is between two wills, those of Samson and of God, whom Samson respects even as he feels that his strength has been the source of his misery and finds his blindness "worse than chains." The verse will continue to express such despair, at least until the arrival of Dalila, because of his sense of having lost the chance to fulfill his destiny. As Samson wrestles with his feelings, he will come to see more clearly despite his moral and physical blindness while progressing toward self-knowledge.

Samson appears as a stationary figure, whose outward stillness belies an inward restlessness and vitality; he contends with weakness, guilt, pride, self-hatred, violence, and despair, seeing no escape from his inner torment except through death. As M. A. Radzinowicz has shown, the hero's long opening speech reveals the intellectual conflict leading to self-discovery. The soliloquy reveals the torments of a divided self, analogous to a pattern found in Job's anxiety and isolation as well as in some of the Psalms; he is a proud, strong hero whose mind is turning against itself and against God.[17] The opening lines focus intensely on Samson, alone, lying in rags, shackled on a dark stage; it is a mood of desolation that might be expected at the climax or conclusion of a tragedy. The great cry, "O dark, dark, dark, amid the blaze of noon" (80), with its counterpointed rhythm, captures the paradox of the future deliverer cut off from God's light. His speech discloses his growing fears of a "living death." He senses the Chorus of Danites, who voice, not Milton's view of events, but the reader's uncertainty and the limited perspective of the hero. Like the others in the play, they come to look at Samson, the hero as spectacle and slave. The Chorus stresses Samson's physical appearance, a sign of his inner state, yet the reader, aware of the story, can see more than the Chorus. The clothing, isolation, and posture suggest Samson's alienation. The Chorus, in words to be echoed by Manoa, points up the contrast between Samson the slave and Samson the folk hero who once made weapons look foolish. The Danites, reflecting Samson's inner turmoil, lament his imprisonment in outward and inward darkness. Samson hears their words yet remains separate on the stage, wrapped in his own thoughts. When the Chorus speaks to him, he starts to revive. Important internal changes are beginning ("the worst now least afflicts me"); his speech of remorse is one of wounded pride, from which hope, the opposite of despair, can come. Samson condemns himself as a fool who divulged his secret gift of God to a deceitful woman. The Chorus not only attacks bad women who have deceived men but reminds the hero not to shift the blame for his state to God. After recalling his first wife, Samson, in a valuable release of hostility, lashes out in anger at his second wife, Dalila, whom he calls a monster and "accomplished snare." Yet recognizing that she was not the prime cause of his fall, he blames his own uxoriousness. The reader, however, wonders why he betrayed God and why Dalila betrayed him. In the Book of Judges (16.16–17) one reads that it was only when Dalila "pressed him daily with her words, and urged him, so that his soul was vexed unto death, that he told her all his heart." Presumably he let himself be tempted; the present action is also a series of temptations, each of which will succeed in stirring the recumbent hero to action. Recounting his battle with the Philistines shows the healing value of speech; as long as he talks, there is hope that despair and depression can turn into positive action, as indicated by the tone of sincere remorse in his speech (290–92) reflecting his recognition that he is the champion of God, not of himself.

The choral theme is central to the play: "Just are the ways of God, / And justifiable to Men." The Chorus attempts to question and defend the mysterious ways of God, raising the issue that Samson was prompted by God to violate one of His own laws. They seem untroubled by the apparent injustice of Samson's being led into temptation without having been strengthened or rescued. No longer doubting that God prompted Samson, they imagine that God is above His own laws since the Danites are unable to explain how one can be commanded to do what is wrong. God, they say, would not have caused this "heroic Nazarite" without reason to seek in marriage a deceitful bride. But the Chorus judges Samson externally and never fully understands the hero, whose greatness is in part revealed by its inadequacy. That Samson is different from ordinary men is also seen in the exchange with his father.

Manoa comes to ransom his son, to offer the kind of comfort and pity that Samson does not want. The father's words are much more effective than his actions; as in the other episodes, the visitor has an effect opposite to what is intended. Those who come to console Samson end up reinforcing his despair, whereas those who come to taunt succeed in rousing him. Each visitor, embodying an aspect of Samson's own problem, comes not only to tempt but also to cure Samson of his spiritual illness. Manoa externalizes his son's accusations against Providence and cures Samson of this fault; Dalila externalizes the hero's weakness and fear, emotions purged by their encounter; and Harapha's comically inflated pride produces a catharsis of Samson's own pride in his strength. Wondering why God granted his request to have a son, Manoa blames God for Samson's plight. Telling his father to trust God, the hero accepts responsibility for the evils that have befallen him. If, as he says, he could have seen through the wiles of Dalila, as he had seen through those of his enemies, one wonders why he gave in. The play raises such basic questions, both about the hero's past and about his present motivation. What mysterious flaw was it that betrayed the strong champion of God? The only explanation he gives to why he succumbed to Dalila is weakness ("foul effeminacy").

In the exchange with Manoa, the poet raises questions about the hero's past: both of Samson's marriages are seen as wrong, even though the first was said to have been God's will. Then, in excited language and syntax, Manoa announces the offstage action of the Philistines' feast in honor of Dagon. To his father's vigorous chastisement, Samson admits that he is guilty of having brought dishonor to his people but hopes that he can show that the true God of the Hebrews is superior to the Philistine god. Acknowledging his sin is the first step in the healing process of repentance; the present state of apparently hopeless passivity will turn into redemptive action. When Manoa announces that he has already attempted to secure his son's ransom, Samson rejects the offer in a mood of pride, anger, and self-pity. Manoa, preferring that this son follow him home, has ironically led Samson close to suicide; at the same time, the hero is moving from indulging in private grief to publicly exercising his God-given heroism. Samson, who does not want to be an object of pity, rejects the comfort of his father, who has tempted the hero to trust him rather than God. Samson acknowledges his own flaw: "swoll'n with pride into the snare I fell." He then tries again to shift the blame to his "deceitful concubine" while admitting to the shame of being "disarm'd among my enemies."

With his father's departure, Samson is at the lowest point in his despair, complaining that Heaven has deserted him; yet hope will come from his obvious strength in surmounting hopelessness. The hero never retreats into silent depression, even when the Chorus reflects his own bafflement at human misery and the mercy of God. Manoa's consolations have led his son to realize his alienation from God; and Samson cries out in a speech (633–51) that shifts from blank verse to alternatingly long and short lines, suggesting the speaker's torment and agony. The Chorus extols the central virtue Samson will come to embody—patience as "the truest fortitude"—then philosophizes about God's mercy and justice, fluctuating in its feelings and reflecting many of Milton's own dark attitudes.

The Chorus announces the arrival of Dalila in an excessively ornate, gaudy description, which, like much of *Samson,* is curiously lacking in color or sharp visual focus, as if imagined inside the blind hero's mind. The reason for her coming is as ambiguous as her motivation. No one knows how truthful she is; she remains inscrutable, her subtlety revealing her past allure. When she claims that wifely affection led her to wish to see her husband once more and to lighten his burden, Samson attacks her as a "Hyaena," his harsh, antifeminist rhetoric reflecting not the poet's view of women but the hero's hatred of his past sin and his fear of the sensuous power that Dalila still has over him. She insists on being heard and cleverly plays on his weakness while ironically asserting the weakness of her sex as the reason for her betrayal of Samson. Dalila claims that she revealed his secret strength to his Philistine enemies lest he leave her. Selfishness is compounded with prevarication when she asserts that those who induced her to tempt Samson planned only his "safe custody" (800); according to the biblical account, the Philistines had asked Dalila to entice Samson's secret so that they might "bind him to afflict him" (Judges 16.5). Dalila's role in the poem is analogous to that of Eve in reversing the fall she occasioned; she inadvertently helps turn self-blame into healing, as Samson's public declaration of responsibility to the Chorus indicates: "I to myself was false ere thou to me." Refusing to forgive her past weakness, Samson has taken the positive action of accepting responsibility for his sin. He listens to her argument that she was coerced by powerful Philistines to betray her husband, that she was forced into a conflict between conscience and public duty. Samson responds with a more carefully reasoned argument on sinning against the sanctity of marriage and "the law of nature." Realizing that she cannot win the argument, Dalila offers to nurse Samson or to intercede for him; but his response to her, as to his father, is one of redoubled resistance; he is now strong enough to insist on his independence. Still struggling against her powerful charms, the proud hero sees Dalila as a temptress who would ensnare him again; to such slavery he prefers the liberty of jail. When she reaches out to touch him, he recoils in a climactic gesture of rage, refusing to return to his past sins; her visit has had the ironic effect of reviving the hero. Seeing that he is implacable, Dalila reveals her self-justification, predicting that her name will be known to all posterity. She departs, still an enigmatic figure of curiosity, desire, regret, self-defense, and anger. As Anthony Low observes, Dalila remains empty beneath her finery, but Samson grows in spiritual stature.[18]

Although Samson contends that she has been sent to debase him, Dalila's visit has managed to uplift him in the psychological development at the heart of the drama. The Chorus, musing on the enigma of human love, returns to its satirically exaggerated antifeminism, which serves to relieve the tension. A final antagonist draws near, a braggart soldier named Harapha, meaning *giant*, whose shallow boasts provide Samson with a reflection of his own vanity. Samson, cutting through Harapha's boasts, ironically castigates the giant's "gorgeous arms." The hero is roused to action, ready to fight with only a staff, more as God's champion than as the primitive tribal strongman Harapha expected. When accused of using magic, Samson significantly responds by asserting that his "trust is in the living God." The hero had earlier thought that the mysterious power in his hair was magical; he now sees that his strength is divinely ordained. The rebirth of the hero, in contrast to his earlier description of himself as a "Sepulcher, a moving Grave" (102), is clear. When Harapha attacks the God of the Israelites, Samson reasserts his faith, and, admitting that he deserves God's just punishment, chooses to be judged by

God, not men. In renewed confidence he challenges Harapha, showing that Samson has recovered his youthful spirit. Samson's unadorned strength triumphs over the martial prowess of his opponent.

When the messenger comes to summon Samson to the Philistine festival, the hero at first says, "I cannot come," because the Hebrew Law prohibits his participation in a pagan rite, the very Law that had forbidden his marriage to Dalila. Yet now he finds the freedom in his heart to obey the divine spirit within him; he thus freely asserts, "I will not come" (1332). The urgings of the Chorus, fearful of disobeying the Law, only confirm Samson in his determination, and he feels his strength returning with his hair. The reader, shifting from Chorus to hero, wondering what action is proper, is relieved by Samson's crucial decision (1372–79). Like Job, Samson learns to obey God, whom he has come to understand, and to reject those human laws that work against man and society. Samson thus discovers through God's mercy a higher law, written in the heart of the believer. He is not free to disobey God "but is freed from obedience to edicts thought to be emanating from God. He is free to obey only the substance of truth."[19] He will go to the temple not because the Law sanctions it or because the Law forbids it since both "may" be possible with God; going is a gesture of freedom and trust in God's power, signified by the "rousing motions" he feels of "something extraordinary." He does not analyze the situation but merely accepts the unlimited possibilities offered by an unknowable God. Here for the first time, the manacled, immobilized hero stands and moves. No longer enslaved by lust or pride, he will follow reason in obeying the Philistine commands, aware of his freedom from the constraint of external laws. He has become the champion of faith, trusting God without knowing whether or not He will approve. The reader knows that this will be Samson's most "remarkable" day as well as his last. The hero going forth to his uncertain fate has the calm assurance of one who, knowing the difference between earthly and heavenly authority, and guided by his conscience, owes obedience only to God. Aware of the possible consequences yet ignorant of the exact outcome, Samson in his action reflects God's will. He freely chooses to meet his destiny, whatever it might be; if this seems to be moral blindness, it is clear that, in terms of the play's inner, spiritual action, he has resolved his conflicts and found peace as well as a greater type of heroic courage. He has completed the journey from darkness to light. With his "inward eyes illuminated," Samson, alone among the characters, truly sees. Like Odeipus, he was blind when he saw; he now sees what he must do, guided by the true light of God that is the voice of conscience.

With the action shifted offstage in the Greek style, Manoa replaces Samson in a kind of subplot. The Chorus becomes anxious and passive, exchanging roles with Samson, who is now the fully active (though unseen) hero. Ironically, Manoa's failure to ransom his son is counterpointed by the success of the main plot; while Samson pays the ransom, Manoa sacrifices all he has to try to ransom his son in an action that fails, whereas the main action succeeds. Manoa speaks of saving his son, even as that son is being destroyed, and cannot see the full mission or victory of Samson. The audience feels renewed sympathy because of the suffering and disillusionment of Manoa, who, with the Chorus, becomes the source of the catharsis.

The messenger rushes in with news of a horrid spectacle: Gaza stands, but "all her Sons are fall'n, / All in a moment overwhelm'd." The hero who has killed the Philistines has himself been killed. The messenger, telling the story of what occurred in the temple, conveys both pity, reflected earlier in Manoa, and fear, reflected in Dalila. He pictures a passive, patient hero who is also active, performing the final action with stupendous force, "as one who pray'd." The final picture of Samson is left ambiguous; one wonders whether he is proud or humble and to what extent he is aware that he is an instrument of Providence. Unlike the biblical Samson, who asks for vengeance, Milton's hero presumably prays that his action will please God. When the messenger describes how the two massive pillars came down, the Chorus rejoices in the "dearly bought revenge, yet glorious" and speaks of Samson "entangled in the fold of dire necessity." Typically, the Danites fail to grasp the significance of Samson's victory and thus of the play's triumphant catastrophe. Stressing the un-Miltonic theme of fatalistic necessity, they miss in the messenger's report the hero's choice to obey "of my own accord" (1643). Manoa, too, overlooks his son's self-discovery and choice to serve God. Samson has rejected the comfortable passivity offered by Manoa and Dalila and has become increasingly aware that the only options open to him are unacceptable. Only when he gives up his independence for dependence on God, surrendering his will to God's, can he resolve his dilemma.

The Chorus, now divided into two parts, speaks of light, into which Samson goes, as into a blaze, and of the more important image of fire, symbolizing Samson as a holocaust and sacrificial victim. Like the legendary phoenix, Samson is reborn in death, triumphant in defeat. The tragic experience is expressed by Manoa, who says that Samson achieved his full humanity in an act of noble heroism. The audience shares in the catharsis by which peace and order as well as justice have been established; yet it has witnessed a profoundly human tragedy. One leaves the play wondering if "all passion" is indeed "spent," if "All is best." The final choral speech points to Samson's religious triumph, his reconciliation with God, but the Chorus also refers to his tragic death as a man who has died and proved himself larger than ordinary men. Providence has made Samson both God's champion and sacrificial victim whose death restores order to the state against which he has sinned.[20] *Samson* thus fulfills the pattern of tragedy as well as the Christian idea of humiliation and self-sacrifice, as represented by Christ the suffering victim, scapegoat, and redeemer, whose death brings eternal life. Samson is great, noble and heroic, as well as pitiable, fearful, and repulsive, a hero whose unheroic attributes humanize and elevate his character. With no earthly weapons and with only a divinely aided will, Samson has been able to execute divine vengeance, exemplifying Milton's ideal of Christian heroism, which is most perfectly embodied in the Christ of *Paradise Regained.*

*Samson* raises numerous doubts and questions, both emotional and intellectual, that are in part resolved by divine Providence working through the hero. Like the Chorus and Manoa, the reader tries but cannot fathom God's mysterious ways yet can trust that God's goodness will ultimately be revealed.[21] Samson hopes that the thoughts stirring in him are prompted by God, yet he must rely on his own wits; as he goes off to the temple, the audience is unable to determine what part of the decision to act is due to his own intuition and what part is due to divine intervention. Readers begin the poem understanding everything because they know the story, yet leave understanding very little. The mystery of God's will remains at the heart of the work: God has willed Samson's "glorious revenge," but one does not know why this has been willed nor what its full significance is.[22] That God remains inscrutable, however, does not mean that He has no plan for humankind; the poem suggests that everything that occurs has a divine explanation. Milton, always adept at exploiting ambiguity, uses uncertainty to bring the readers closer to the action, forcing them to explore its mysteries, to look beyond the surface plot. *Samson* is a powerful drama whose originality comes from its brilliant synthesis of Greek, Hebrew, and Christian elements and from the integration of recurrent themes in Milton's work—temptation, obedience, freedom, and patient endurance—with the poet's mature tragic vision.

# Conclusion: Milton's Reputation

Milton remains more controversial than any other major English writer. In his own time, his works were widely praised, quoted, and attacked both at home and abroad. Since then, they have sparked some of the most valuable literary criticism and have influenced artists in various media. *Paradise Lost,* consistently in print in many editions and in many languages, has become a standard against which major poetry is judged, in part because every major critic has interpreted it and because many great poets—Dryden, Pope, Blake, Wordsworth, Shelley, Byron, Keats, Tennyson, Hopkins, among others—have imitated, or been influenced by, its style and sublimity.

With his concern for universal order and human virtue, Milton, like Dante, has been considered the preeminent Christian poet, regarded by some readers as almost canonical as the Bible. Since it reflected popular beliefs, *Paradise Lost* was long regarded as the major religious poem in English. In fact, however, Milton was an unorthodox Christian more concerned with establishing a just society on earth than with defining supernatural mysteries or eternal rewards. Unlike most religious poets, he was less interested in analyzing the meaning of personal salvation than in wrestling with moral and intellectual issues. As Hill observes, Milton never resolved the tension in him between liberty and discipline, passion and reason, human love and divine Providence, the needs of individuals and of society.[1] Milton the man remains a complex personality. The image he fostered of himself as an aloof intellectual has reinforced the stereotype of the poet as a sour Puritan, an arrogant male chauvinist. In fact, as a thinker, he is too elusive to be accurately labeled and as a poet too original.

Milton's voice has always been too powerful to be ignored. Dryden, who in 1688 elevated Milton to the pantheon of heroic poets, after Homer and Virgil, indicated the direction of later criticism by seeing *Paradise Lost* as the standard for judging great poetry. More important was Joseph Addison's detailed analysis of the epic in the *Spectator* (1712), which enhanced the reputation of the poet as the greatest English writer because of his handling of the greatest literary form, the epic. Samuel Johnson's *Life of Milton* (1779) then became the basis for most later evaluations. Despite his rationalist prejudices and numerous reservations, Johnson honestly confessed that Milton's power triumphs over the dictates of neoclassical decorum: "criticism," he wrote, "sinks in admiration."[2]

Milton, then, was established early as a fixture in English literature. Having mastered the noblest genres and having synthesized disparate traditions, he was a modern classic, England's national poet, a giant of the recent past whose life had been uncommonly tied to that of the nation. Milton helped to stimulate some of the best poetry of the eighteenth century and to set the poetic agenda for that period, when much of the best verse was a response to his work.[3]

Pope, Johnson, Addison, and others tended to concentrate on Milton's ideas, considering the man as repulsive as his political views. But, in fact, the separation of Milton the poet and Milton the politician is impossible to make. The writer himself emphasized the essential link between his life and works. As a result, many critics over the centuries have combined their admiration for Milton with numerous reservations and qualifications because of a dislike for the poet's Christianity, politics, or character. It was not easy for many readers to forgive the propagandist of the Revolution and defender of regicide. Whereas the Victorians tended to dislike Milton the man and his subversive politics and theology, the Romantics, impressed by the greatness of the poet's mind and his influence, generally took a more balanced view of the man, thinker, and poet. As Wittreich tells us, early nineteenth-century poets tended to see Milton as majestic, sublime, and solemn, as an artist seriously dedicated to virtue, as a daring individualist, not arrogant but with an aloofness bespeaking his spiritual superiority.[4] Even when disapproving of Milton's politics, the Romantics admired his constancy in the face of adversity. Blake considered Milton England's greatest poet and savior, whose task was to awaken Europe to the deepest truths about religion and politics, whose unconventional views were seen as heroic and prophetic. Shelley, Byron, and other Romantics saw the Satan of *Paradise Lost* as an admirable, sympathetic hero just as they celebrated his creator as the great rebel-artist. Such commentators minimized Milton's theological views, overvalued his style and feeling, and thus esteemed the poet for reflecting their own biases. Still, they were better able than many eighteenth-century critics to grasp the true achievement of Milton and thus gave him a veneration accorded no other poet. As a man, Milton captured what the Romantics most admired, and as a poet he reflected their aesthetic ideals: Milton was a radical, a republican, and a rebel who was also a classical poet, a lofty thinker, and a man of action.

In the twentieth century, Milton has been the source of ongoing, often controversial, scrutiny. No major work has been so vigorously challenged and defended by influential critics as *Paradise Lost*. T. S. Eliot and Ezra Pound, among others, criticized Milton as a bad influence on language and poetry, largely because his style was irrelevant to their own poetic purposes. Critics such as F. R. Leavis, and A. J. A. Waldock found serious fault with *Paradise Lost,* in part because they discounted its religious ideas. More recently, Milton's work has been examined from a variety of critical perspectives that have revealed new aspects of the poet's complex artistry. Milton's reputation as one of the world's great poets has never been questioned, and his subtle originality and considerable beauty are more fully appreciated with each critical evaluation. Sometimes called the last Elizabethan, Milton was also the last, and greatest, embodiment of the English Renaissance, an idealist for whom poetry was not a pastime or amusement but the most sacred human activity. Thoroughly assimilating his sources into his own unique synthesis, he produced the major classical epic in English as well as the finest "Greek" tragedy, restored the vitality of the pastoral, transformed the masque, extended the scope of the sonnet and of blank verse, and developed a style that has proved both influential and inimitable. Moreover, Milton raised many of the enduring human questions concerning the nature of God, freedom, evil, love, and virtue and defended the value of reason with eloquence and power.

# Notes

## Chapter 1: Milton's Life and Times

1. Basil Willey, *The Seventeenth Century Background* (Garden City, NY: Doubleday, 1953), p. 50.
2. Christopher Hill, *Milton and the English Revolution* (New York: Viking, 1977), p. 4.
3. A. N. Wilson, *The Life of John Milton* (New York: Oxford, 1984), p. 11.
4. Ibid., p. 121.
5. James Thorpe, *John Milton: The Inner Life* (San Marino, CA: Huntington Library, 1983), p. 56.
6. David Daiches, *Milton* (New York: Norton, 1957), p. 110.
7. Hugh Trevor-Roper, "Milton in Politics," in *Catholics, Anglicans and Puritans: Seventeenth Century Essays* (Chicago: University of Chicago Press. 1987), p. 253.
8. James Holly Hanford, *Milton Handbook,* 4th ed. (New York: Appleton, 1954), p. 173.
9. Hanford, p. 171.
10. Hill, p. 57.
11. John Carey, *Milton* (London: Evans, 1969), p. 21.
12. Hill, p. 197.
13. William Riley Parker, *Milton: A Biography,* vol. 1 (Oxford: Clarendon Press, 1968), p. 571.
14. Thorpe, p. 71.
15. Thorpe, p. 75.

## Chapter 2: "The Lofty Rhyme"

1. J. B. Leishman, *Milton's Minor Poems* (London: Hutchinson, 1969), p. 52.

2. Hugh Maclean, "Milton's *Fair Infant,*" in *ELH* 24 (1957): 296–303; reprint in *Milton: Modern Essays in Criticism,* ed. A. E. Barker (Oxford: Oxford University Press, 1965), p. 22.

3. Merritt Y. Hughes, ed., *John Milton: Complete Poems and Major Prose* (New York: Odyssey, 1957), p. 46.

4. Leishman, p. 80.

5. Leishman, p. 83.

6. Marjorie H. Nicolson, *John Milton: A Reader's Guide to His Poetry* (New York: Farrar, Straus, and Giroux, 1963), p. 53.

7. Rosemond Tuve, "Structural Figures of *L'Allegro* and *I1 Penseroso,*" in *Images and Themes in Five Poems by Milton* (Cambridge: Harvard University Press, 1957), pp. 15–36, reprint in *Milton: Modern Essays in Criticism,* ed. A. E. Barker (Oxford: Oxford University Press, 1957), p. 58.

8. Nicolson, p. 59.

9. Leishman, p. 137.

10. Tuve, p. 61.

11. Archie Burnett, *Milton's Style* (London: Longman, 1981), p. 18.

12. Rosemond Tuve, "The Symbol of Light in *Comus,*" in *Images and Themes in Five Poems by Milton* (Cambridge: Harvard University Press, 1957); reprint in *Milton: "Comus" and "Samson Agonistes,"* ed. Julian Lovelock (London: Macmillan, 1975), p. 77.

13. J. B. Broadbent, "Pastoral in *Comus,*" in *Milton: "Comus" and "Samson Agonistes,"* ed. Julian Lovelock (London: Macmillan, 1975), p. 72.

14. C. L. Barber, "*A Mask Presented at Ludlow Castle:* The Masque as Masque," in *Milton: "Comus" and "Samson Agonistes,"* ed. Julian Lovelock (London: Macmillan, 1975), p. 98.

15. Balachandra Rajan, *The Lofty Rhyme* (London: Routlege and Kegan Paul, 1970), p. 37.

16. Rajan, p. 44.

17. Rajan, p. 27.

18. Roger B. Wilkenfeld, "The Seat at the Center: An Interpretation of *Comus,* in *Critical Essays on Milton from "ELH"* (Baltimore: John Hopkins University Press, 1969), p. 125.

19. Rosemond Tuve, "Theme, Pattern, and Imagery in *Lycidas,*" in *Milton's "Lycidas": The Tradition and the Poem,* ed. C. A. Patrides (Columbia: University of Missouri Press, 1983), p. 171.

20. Joseph A. Wittreich, Jr., *Visionary Poetics* (San Marino: Huntington Library, 1979), p. 167.

21. Burnett, p. 87.

22. Tuve, "Theme," p. 192.

23. Burnett, p. 85.

24. Rajan, p. 53.

## Chapter 3: *Paradise Lost*

1. John M. Steadman, *Milton and the Renaissance Hero* (Oxford: Clarendon, 1967), p. 174.

2. John T. Shawcross, *With Mortal Voice* (Lexington: University of Kentucky Press, 1982), p. 41.

3. James L. Thorpe, ed., *Milton Criticism* (New York: Rinehart, 1950), p. 320.

4. Shawcross, p. 101.

5. Arnold Stein, *Answerable Style* (Seattle: University of Washington Press, 1967), p. 137.

6. Rajan, *Lofty Rhyme*, p. 102.

7. Joseph H. Summers, *The Muse's Method* (Cambridge: Harvard University Press, 1962), p. 23.

8. C. S. Lewis, *A Preface to "Paradise Lost"* (Oxford: Oxford University Press, 1960), p. 40.

9. C. M. Bowra, *From Virgil to Milton* (London: Macmillan, 1945), p. 198.

10. Christopher Ricks, *Milton's Grand Style* (Oxford: Clarendon, 1963), pp. 59–60.

11. Stein, p. 151.

12. J. B. Broadbent, *"Paradise Lost": Introductions* (Cambridge: Cambridge University Press, 1973), p. 145.

13. Broadbent, p. 146.

14. Lewis, p. 67.

15. Lewis, p. 67

16. Douglas Bush, *"Paradise Lost" in Our Time* (New York: Smith, 1957), p. 37.

17. Summers, p. 11.

18. Louis L. Martz, *Poet of Exile* (New Haven: Yale University Press, 1980), p. 107.

19. Merritt Y. Hughes, ed., *John Milton: Complete Poems and Major Prose* (New York: Odyssey, 1957), p. 182.

20. Lewis, p. 94.

21. Hughes, pp. 183–84.

22. Harry Blamires, *Milton's Creation* (London: Methuen, 1971), p. 43.

23. Marjorie Hope Nicolson, "Milton and the Telescope," in *ELH*, 2 (1935): 1–32; reprint in *Critical Essays on Milton from "ELH"* (Baltimore: Johns Hopkins University Press,1969), p. 29.

24. Michael J. Lieb, *Poetics of the Holy* (Chapel Hill: University of North Carolina Press, 1981), p. 203.

25. Stanley Fish, *Surprised by Sin* (New York: Macmillan, 1967), pp. 74–75.

26. Rajan, p. 71.
27. Blamires, p. 72.
28. Hughes, p. 272.
29. Hughes, p. 285.
30. Blamires, p. 113.
31. George Williamson, "The Education of Adam," in *Modern Philology,* 61 (1963): 96–109; reprint in A. E. Barker, ed., *Milton: Modern Essays in Criticism* (New York: Oxford, 1965), p. 285.
32. Blamires, p. 134.
33. Albert C. Labriola, " 'Thy Humiliation Shall Exalt': The Christology of *Paradise Lost,*" in *Milton Studies,* 15 (1981): 29–42.
34. Stella P. Revard, *The War in Heaven* (Ithaca: Cornell University Press, 1980), p. 80.
35. Hughes, p. 332.
36. Blamires, p. 176.
37. Blamires, p. 178.
38. Nicolson, p. 45.
39. Hughes, p. 393.
40. Hughes, p. 416.
41. Blamires, p. 268.
42. G. K. Hunter, *Paradise Lost* (London: Allen and Unwin, 1980), p. 153.
43. Summers, p. 190.
44. Mary Ann Radzinowicz, " 'Man as a Probationer of Immortality': *Paradise Lost* XI–XII," in *Approaches to Paradise Lost,* ed. C. A. Patrides (Toronto: University of Toronto Press, 1980), pp. 36–37.
45. Hunter, p. 156.
46. Hunter, p. 161.
47. Hughes, p. 461.

## Chapter 4: *Paradise Regained* and *Samson Agonistes*

1. John T. Shawcross, *Paradise Regain'd* (Pittsburgh: Duquesne University Press, 1988), p. 104.
2. Christopher Hill, *The Experience of Defeat: Milton and Some Contemporaries* (New York: Viking, 1984), p. 315.
3. William B. Hunter, Jr., "The Obedience of Christ in *Paradise Regained,*" in *Calm of Mind: Tercentenary Essays on "Paradise Regained" and "Samson Agonistes" in Honor of John S. Diekhoff,* ed. Joseph Anthony Wittreich, Jr. (Cleveland: Case Western Reserve University Press, 1971), p. 69.
4. Barbara K. Lewalski, *Milton's Brief Epic* (Providence: Brown University Press, 1966), pp. 18–25.

5. Jon S. Lawry, *The Shadow of Heaven* (Ithaca: Cornell University Press, 1968), p. 292.

6. Lewalski, p. 159.

7. Lawry, p. 295.

8. Stanley E. Fish, "Inaction and Silence: The Reader in *Paradise Regained*," in *Calm of Mind*, ed. J. A. Wittreich, Jr. (Cleveland: Case Western Reserve University Press, 1971), p. 38.

9. Burton O. Kurth, *Milton and Christian Heroism* (Hamden: Shoe String, 1966).

10. Rajan, p. 119.

11. Rajan, p. 124.

12. Shawcross, p. 2.

13. Mary Ann Radzinowicz, *Toward "Samson Agonistes"* (Princeton: Princeton University Press, 1978), p. 167.

14. Hughes, p. 544.

15. A. S. P. Woodhouse, "Tragic Effect in *Samson Agonistes*," in *University of Toronto Quarterly*, 28 (1958–59): 205–22; reprint in *Milton: Modern Essays in Criticism*, ed. A. E. Barker (Oxford: Galaxy, 1965), p. 464.

16. William G. Madsen, "From Shadowy Types to Truth," in *Twentieth Century Interpretations of "Samson Agonistes,"* ed. G. M. Crump (Englewood Cliffs: Prentice-Hall, 1968), p. 95.

17. Radzinowicz, p. 21.

18. Anthony Low, *The Blaze of Noon* (New York: Columbia University Press, 1974), p. 98.

19. Radzinowicz, p. 262.

20. Low, p. 56.

21. Low, p. 92.

22. Stanley Fish, "Question and Answer in *Samson Agonistes* (1969)," in *Milton: "Comus" and "Samson Agonistes,"* ed. Julian Lovelock (London: Macmillan, 1975), p. 238.

## Conclusion

1. Christopher Hill, *Milton and the English Revolution* (New York: Viking, 1977), p. 464.

2. Samuel Johnson, *Lives of the Poets*, ed. George Birbeck Hill (Oxford: Clarendon, 1905), I.190.

3. Dustin Griffin, *Regaining Paradise* (Cambridge: Cambridge University Press, 1986), p. 2.

4. Joseph Wittreich, Jr., ed. *The Romantics on Milton* (Cleveland: Case Western Reserve University Press, 1970), p. 11.

# Select Bibliography


Adams, Robert M. *Ikon: John Milton and the Modern Critics.* Ithaca: Cornell University Press, 1966.

Barker, Arthur, ed. *Milton: Modern Essays in Criticism.* New York: Oxford University Press, 1965.

Berry, Boyd M. *Process of Speech: Puritan Religious Writing and "Paradise Lost."* Baltimore: Johns Hopkins University Press, 1976.

Blamires, Harry. *Milton's Creation: A Guide Through "Paradise Lost."* London: Methuen, 1971.

Blessington, Francis C. *"Paradise Lost" and the Classical Epic.* London: Routledge, 1979.

Bowra, C. M. *From Virgil to Milton.* London: Macmillan, 1945.

Broadbent, John B. *Some Graver Subject: An Essay on "Paradise Lost."* 1960. London: Schocken, 1967.

Burnett, Archie. *Milton's Style.* London: Longman, 1981.

Bush, Douglas. *"Paradise Lost" in Our Time: Some Comments.* New York: Smith, 1957.

Carey, John. *Milton.* London: Evans, 1969.

Cope, Jackson I. *The Metaphoric Structure of "Paradise Lost."* Baltimore: Johns Hopkins University Press, 1962.

Daniells, Roy. *Milton, Mannerism, and Baroque.* Toronto: University of Toronto Press, 1963.

Darbishire, Helen. *Milton's "Paradise Lost."* Oxford: Clarendon Press, 1951.

Davies, Stevie. *Images of Kingship in "Paradise Lost."* Columbia: University of Missouri Press, 1983.

Demaray, John G. *Milton and the Masque Tradition.* Cambridge: Harvard University Press, 1968.

———. *Milton's Theatrical Epic: The Invention and Design of "Paradise Lost."* Cambridge: Harvard University Press, 1980.

Diekhoff, John S. *Milton's "Paradise Lost": A Commentary on the Argument.* New York: Humanities, 1958.

Eliot, T. S. "Milton I." *On Poetry and Poets*. London: Faber, 1957. 138–45.

Empson, William. *Milton's God*. London: Chatto, 1965.

Evans, J. M. *"Paradise Lost" and the Genesis Tradition*. London: Oxford University Press, 1968.

Ferry, Anne Davidson. *Milton's Epic Voice: The Narrator in "Paradise Lost."* Cambridge: Harvard University Press, 1963.

Fish, Stanley. *Surprised by Sin: The Reader in "Paradise Lost."* New York: Macmillan, 1967.

Fixler, Michael. *Milton and the Kingdoms of God*. Evanston: Northwestern University Press, 1964.

Fletcher, Harris F. *The Intellectual Development of John Milton*. 2 vols. Urbana: University of Illinois Press, 1956, 1962.

French, J. M., comp. *The Life Records of John Milton*. 5 vols. New Brunswick: Rutgers University Press, 1949–58.

Frye, Northrop. *The Return to Eden: Five Essays on Milton's Epics*. Toronto: University of Toronto Press, 1965.

Frye, Roland Mushat. *Milton's Imagery and the Visual Arts: Iconographic Tradition in the Epic Poems*. Princeton: Princeton University Press, 1978.

Gardner, Helen. *A Reading of "Paradise Lost."* Oxford: Oxford University Press, 1965.

Grose, Christopher. *Milton's Epic Process: "Paradise Lost" and Its Miltonic Background*. New Haven: Yale University Press, 1973.

Hill, Christopher. *Milton and the English Revolution*. New York: Viking, 1977.

Hill, John Spencer. *John Milton, Poet, Prophet, Priest*. Totowa, N.J.: Rowman & Littlefield, 1979.

Honigmann, E. A. J. *Milton's Sonnets*. New York: St. Martin's, 1966.

Huckabay, Calvin. *John Milton: An Annotated Bibliography, 1929–1968*. Rev. ed. Pittsburgh: Duquesne University Press, 1970.

Hughes, Merritt Y. *Ten Perspectives on Milton*. New Haven: Yale University Press, 1965.

———, and John Steadman, eds. *A Variorum Commentary on the Poems of John Milton*. 4 vols. to date. New York: Columbia University Press, 1972.

Hunter, G. K. *"Paradise Lost."* London: Allen & Unwin, 1980.

Hunter, William B., Jr., C. A. Patrides, and J. H. Adamson. *Bright Essence: Studies in Milton's Theology*. Salt Lake City: University of Utah Press, 1971.

———, John T. Shawcross, and John M. Steadman, eds. *A Milton Encyclopedia*. 8 vols. Lewisburg: Bucknell University Press, 1978–79.

Knott, John R., Jr. *Milton's Pastoral Vision: An Approach to "Paradise Lost."* Chicago: University of Chicago Press, 1971.

# INDEX